THE *Head* & THE
——PRESS——
EST. 2012

the first

RUST BELT RISING

Almanac

Spring 2013

COLLECTED, EDITED AND PUBLISHED BY
THE HEAD & THE HAND PRESS, PHILADELPHIA, PENNSYLVANIA

The Head & The Hand Press's

RUST BELT RISING

ALMANAC

With a Copyright for the year being

2013:

*Of matters Curious, Useful, and Entertaining to the
People of The Rust Belt & Beyond*

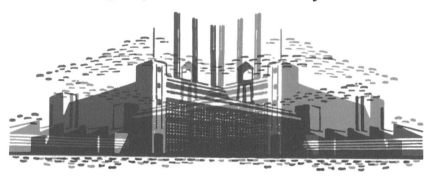

From creation, here be it, that all rights shall be reserved by The Head & The Hand Press. Whereas no part
of this publication may be transmitted, transposed, replicated or reproduced by waves of any means both radio
and digital over both land and sea without consent by correspondence from the publisher. Herein all requests
for reproducing any part of the work both in the printed form and through modern means of technology must
be made expressly and without delay to the publisher.

Cover Art and Layout in Philadelphia, Pennsylvania by Carpe Diem Construction Co.

Printed in Dexter, Michigan by Thomson Shore

Published in Philadelphia, Pennsylvania by The Head & The Hand Press

www.theheadandthehand.com

www.therustbeltrisingalmanac.com

ISBN: 978-0-9893125-0-9

LETTER *from the* EDITOR

I sincerely thought that when The Head & The Hand Press first approached me to edit their forthcoming *Rust Belt Rising Almanac*, the invitation was due to my Doctorate in Sociology with an emphasis on Ethnography (and the accompanying doctoral dissertation "Gentrification and Being in Williamsburg"), my first masters in Urban Geography, my second masters in Urban Anthropology, my dual undergraduate degree in Urban Studies and Studies of Urban People, my YouTube lecture series on Gender, Race and Class in High School Girls Field Hockey, and my most recent endeavor, publishing my own quarterly, *Being Gluten Free in America: The Oppression of an Entire Eating Class.*

I must also admit that I considered refusing their request. The prospect of collaborating with a small press did little to pique my interest. And the fact that their only title was a pseudo-biographical manifesto masquerading as literature on a topic as impractical and unproved as urban farming, written by their founder no less, had me drafting my declination letter. Had my research grant to study the effects of reading Romantic poetry aloud to street dogs in Mexico City remained fully funded, I probably wouldn't have taken the offer.

But here I am, sitting in their basement offices that they've so quaintly dubbed "The Workshop." "Meat locker" would have been more appropriate considering the way the cold from the concrete floor is seeping into my metatarsals. Thank goodness someone had the sense to put sheet rock up—I try not to imagine what condition the bricks of this building are in and what creatures are inhabiting the crevices. While I was writing my doctoral dissertation, I surmised that if gentrification was inevitable, then at least the damned buildings would have heat.

But I digress. I truly believed that my aforementioned magnum opus would be the exempli gratia, the pièce de résistance capable of directing this project toward something that would make Wittgenstein, Heidegger, and Weber proud. I declared my intent to tell the story of the Rust Belt by utilizing the keen analytical eye of the academic. It was not easy to wrestle away the submissions from the totalitarian capitalists that run this company, but I did. And I only had to read one before I wished that I never had.

My mea culpa came while reading the story "What Sort of Girls Wear Lipstick These Days?" How would I ever explain sanctioning such Kerouacian chauvinism to my colleagues in the women's studies department? A young man, driving across the Midwest on some Quixotic quest to Philadelphia of all places, lacing the narrative with disparaging witticisms about the woman he left and the gas station attendants he encounters. I must admit, I did suppress a chuckle when he contemplated the note he would write after riding the elevator to the top of the Gateway Arch. But how can I justify this temporary lapse in sensitivity to my inner feminist?

Then there was "Pebbles" (a seemingly innocuous title), a story that utterly refutes every shred of data found in clinical studies pertaining to the theories of co-dependency and addiction. I'm not sure if the author meant this as a double entendre, but analyzing the title of the story in relation to what happens to the story's antagonist, let's just say, does not bode well for someone who possesses both an X and Y chromosome.

Submission after submission, I experienced these Rust Belt cities in a way that my grad school-guided field tours—even my course work as an ethnographer—could never have prepared me. I felt the uneasiness of staring through a chain-link fence. I choked on the fumes spewing from the factory outside of Pittsburgh that the manufacturing-minded Keynesian economists believe will lead our society back to its previous glory. And dare I say I felt a certain affinity for the *je ne sais quoi* of the streetwalkers captured by Jeffrey Stockbridge's lens.

Despite the degree of skepticism years of study at elite institutions will breed in a scholar, I could not help but feel a guarded optimism that the Rust Belt is in fact rising. Yes, as reductionist as it may be, Cleveland is a vocation for a person willing to forgo personal gain to serve his fellow citizens. Yes, it is inspiring that even with a serial killer at large, a young photographer will return to the place her family once lived to prove that they did not toil in the factories for naught. Yes, sports may be completely sexist, barbaric, and oppressive, but I can now understand why spectators stand and cheer when a team from one of these downtrodden cities actually wins. And yes, above all theories

of gentrification and class and race, ice cream may well be the triumphus maximus for the revival of America's Rust Belt Cities.

If I'm being honest with myself, the ivory towers of academia and the condescending, bourgeois criticism echoing within can take a flying leap. Or rather, the critics can take a flying leap off of said towers. Damn it, I feel reborn. I do not need to hide the fact that I may actually find more satisfaction constructing one of the desks in The Head & The Hand's Workshop than constructing a vicious refutation of a fellow colleague's research. Or that I experience more mental stimulation while talking to a geriatric from the neighborhood than I do discussing socio-economic policy with a GA. Or that I sometimes like to indulge in a 2 a.m. egg roll from the Chinese takeout place with the three-inch thick glass window at the counter underneath the El. Maybe I'll never go back. Maybe I'll just stay here in Kensington. Maybe I'll buy a shell, learn how to hang sheet rock to hide the creatures in the crevices, and start a new life. Maybe I'll discontinue my account with the university grant-finding database and willingly join the ranks of the highly educated who are taking jobs for less pay and more fulfillment. Maybe this is the start of my new life in the Rust Belt.

I wonder if Little Baby's Ice Cream is hiring.

Yours,

Jaheymus Joyce Zeit-Geistman

Jaheymus Joyce Zeit-Geistman

Chronology

1732 – Benjamin Franklin publishes "Poor Ric[...]

Johannes Gutenberg creates the printing press – 1450

1838 – St. John's Episcopal Church is built in C[...]

London confectioner Philip Lenzi opens first American ice cream parlor in New York City, NY – 1774

1897 – Charles M. Schwab, at the age o[...]

Karl Marx publishes The Communist Manifesto –1848

1917 – Female factory workers con[...]

First Model T is made at the Ford Motor Company in Detroit, MI – 1908

1952 – Levitt & Sons build [...]

Bethlehem Steel Company opens a subsidiary in Lackawanna, NY, just outside Buffalo – 1922

1961 – John F. Kenned[...]

Motown Records is established in Detroit, MI with the opening of Hitsville, USA – 1960

1962 – Rachel Ca[...]

First Walmart opens – 1962

1971 – Stets[...]

GenOn power plant opens eighteen miles outside of Pittsburgh, PA – 1970

1973 – [...]

First known use of the phrase "Rust Belt" (arguably) – 1983

19[...]

Motown moves headquarters to Los Angeles, CA, shutting down all operations in Detroit, MI – 1972

Philadelphia's Mural Arts Program begins – 1984

One Liberty Place is built in Philadelphia, PA with a height surpassing that of William Penn atop City Hall – 19[...]

A former American Greetings factory is converted into 78th Street Studios in Cleveland, O[...]

The intersection at Kensington Avenue and Somerset Street is named as the worst drug corner in Philadelphia V[...]

Little Baby's begins to sell ice cream out of a tricycle cart in Phil[...]

...nack" in Philadelphia, PA

...president of the Carnegie Steel Company

...on poisoning at the United States Radium Factory in Orange, NJ

...A as a complete community, creating the first suburb

...s President of the United States hatless; hats go out of style

...Silent Spring

...any plant in the Kensington neighborhood of Philadelphia, PA shuts down as a result of decreased demand for hats

...ses foreign cars to take over a larger share of United States auto market

...em Steel Company closes its Lackawanna, PA branch

...rack is "used on a large scale in urban populations across the United States

...3 – Trumbullplex, an "anarchist housing collective," is founded in Detroit, MI

2007 – St. John's closes as a worship space

2008 – Philadelphia Phillies win the World Series, only the second time in the history of the oldest professional sports franchise in the United States

2011

2012 – Springdale, PA residents file lawsuit against GenOn plant as a community nuisance

7

Here – 2013

TRADEMARKS

Kim Geralds

Hands callused and meaty, mix
mortar—sand, lime and cement
lay brick upon brick, leveled and plumb

Hands mashed, two fingertips lost
stamp fenders of galvanized steel, in
2.4 minutes, rushed down the line

Hands stained by tobacco, shift
ten gears and drive truck, haul
gravel or lumber, axles or Chevys

Hands blackened, grease under
nails, knuckles scraped raw, repairs
by wrench, torque and muscle

Hands floured white with cement
screed, float and edge the mud
smooth, broom in the finish

Hands numbed, the chainsaw revs
its two-stroke song, a hundred
year tree, lay fallen in pieces

Hands callused and meaty, marked
by the work, lay brick upon brick
plumb, level and true

WILLOW STREET STEAM PLANT

K-Fai Steele

POEM WRITTEN IN A CHAIN-LINK FENCE
Sean Thomas Dougherty

I can't help but ask for the honey
   from the wild bees, who can refuse me?
And the choreography of birds.
   What is the light but a form of farewell?
The old women bending into the earth.
   For the body inside our body
is the light is the bread is the wafer
   of moon through the orchard of olive trees,
the olives with that light
   or who resurrects us with a note
or a word, live-it-up-shake-that-thing
   becoming a noise that turns on
and off like that sign of Lebron
   and they triumph as we fail, we recall
a voice heard before despair
   and even the old men
sitting on stoops playing dominoes
   look up, wearing their wreaths.
And anger is not a pushing away
   from ourselves, but into ourselves,

with each blow we are trying
   to hide like the square
inside a rectangle, a system
   of blocks, invisible red markers,
might as well erect barriers,
   lay our pylons at Sojourner Truth
Hair Salon, the corner store
   stocked with 40s, Spray tanned
Russian chicks, neon Chicken,
   as the symphony stutters the failure
of this city could be its triumph
   no free parking but the meter maids
dancing handing out free quarters
   and menthols, and at the corner
red light windshield washers
   singing "My Girl." The Columbian
gold chained gangsters drenched
   in cologne, strutting, trash-talking
ballers behind chain-link fences,
   glorious: Our mothers rising
early for work. Glorious.

Our fathers coming home
at dawn from work. Glorious.
    Refugees from Somalia, Iraq, Sudan,
Guatemala, Mexico, Eritrea,
    Croatia, the ice cream truck man
selling dope with popsicles,
    counter girls and fast food
delivery boys all making jack
    shit for wages. A clenched fist
Is not an asking but a spark
    So set it off to the left ya'll,
set it off to the right of the detectives
    knocking on your front door,
who never notice this earthworm,
    the size of my finger. Digging
into the dirt I sigh
    and am overcome by a feeling close
to love like saffron. Or the sea.
    Or the wind of other evenings
blessed as salt. An incandescence
    beyond anger. The wick of joy.

left: REMEMBER; *Right:* CYCLES OF THE MUSE

Cindy LaFerle

On

JOHN GEORGE BOYCE

An Interview with Denis Boyce

LINDA GALLANT

photography by DANETTE PASCARELLA *except where noted*

I used to live around the corner from a gated garden. More specifically, a gated sculpture garden populated by welded cats, cubes, and jagged profiles that survey the corner of Frankford Avenue and Mercer Street in Fishtown, Philadelphia. My sister Amanda became friendly with Denis Boyce, the garden's creator and owner of Karlie, an art and antique store on the same block as the garden. As the far less outgoing sibling, my interactions with Denis never progressed beyond head nods and waves as I walked my dog past his place, making sure Charlie didn't mark the tulip border or the metal rose petal candle holders lining the low brick wall along the gallery's exterior (welded there by his father John, I later found out). I was a silent admirer, a below average Fishtown denizen, not exactly detracting from my environment but not really contributing either. Still, I wanted to know more about the garden, a standout in a neighborhood known more for its crime stats and alcoholism rates than its arts initiatives.

I convinced my sister, another artist, to join me in a well-intentioned ambush. We found Denis arranging furniture out on the sidewalk alongside his daughter Heather who runs the 20th Century by HKFA (Heather Karlie Fine Art) gallery space next to his. Our conversation quickly turned to stories about his father, John George Boyce, the artist, teacher, and mathematician whose welded sculptures make this slice of Fishtown different in the best sense of the word. Beginning with John's sculptures, three generations of artisans form a row along this stretch of Frankford Avenue.

courtesy of DENIS BOYCE

I. Zigs and Zags

LG: What first motivated you to take over the lot?

DB: Well, I didn't do it for Fishtown. This isn't a nice story that you're writing.

LG: It's O.K. that it's not a nice story. Why not for Fishtown?

DB: Well, back in the '80's and '90's when things started changing—I'm talking the 25-45-year-old demographic coming in—they were mostly assholes. No offense. [Laughter. Mostly mine.] What I liked, one nice thing, was that the suits and the crackwhores would all have the same reaction as they walked by the garden. I started building this thing for my dad a long time ago. They would wander down the street and

be ecstatic I was doing it. They wanted something to look at. The point being that what they said made them all human beings. We're all the same. But I didn't do it for them. I didn't have the city haul away the burned-out cars and the dead bodies for anyone but my dad. It's like, everyone that used to sit out here in front of the Fishtown Tavern, they're all dead. I'm here because I don't drink and I don't do drugs, but I'm of that tribe. You wouldn't know because you're a white girl from the suburbs, but that's what it was like for us. People would get up in the morning and start drinking a six pack, they'd pour beer on their cereal because there wasn't any milk in the fridge.

LG: Well, we know something about that. [My sister snorts in affirmation.]

DB: I've been drunk before, you've been drunk

before, she's been drunk before [points to Amanda] but these guys, the loads, are just paralyzed by it. One guy had three liver transplants.

LG: So, do you think these groups are doomed to be oil and water out here, the 25-45-year-old assholes and the loads or...

DB: No, because they all die.

LG: How long do they live?

DB: Forties. If that. I used to step over the people out here, it was like Brazil in the '80's. At least here the cops came. It's something someone like yourself would never know.

LG: What about these businesses here? [I point to the recently opened Bottle Bar across the street.] Who would you be happy to call a neighbor?

DB: Don't get me wrong, I like those guys. I like Brad and Mike, they're genius, entrepreneur heroes of mine. But when they first started, I was actually concerned for them. I asked them if they were sure they wanted all those varieties of beers in there. Privately I was thinking, you know, *Good luck with that*. How wrong could I have been? I see lines out the door everyday now. But I like your sister, I like Brad and Mike, they're nice, your dog's nice. Things are changing with the younger crowd around here, they come into the shop and some of them know what they're talking about. But I can't give you a nice story about Fishtown.

LG: Still, people like you are making an impact.

DB: Don't give me too much credit. I'm not a visionary, I just made a good buy at the right time. I don't care about... [he makes a wide, arc-ing gesture with his hands]. People will come in with investors and point to my place as evidence of an up-and-coming neighborhood. Yes and no. There are still families here with bad problems, drugs and alcohol, but they hold down jobs and get married and have kids. The kids zig when they should have zagged. You have friends like that don't you? The crackwhores didn't get on the El and head towards center city, they stayed here.

II. Chubby Checker, IBM, and Pure Silver

LG: Would it be alright to see the sculptures up close?

Denis nods and unlocks the padlock on the gate. We step through and walk toward my favorite sculpture, a cat whose arching hindquarters salute the facing stretch of Frankford. The handworked metal sheet plunged into the dirt next to the base reads "Plato's Cat." He reaches out and touches the long, attenuated beam connected to the sculpture labeled "Three Kings" and it slowly, soundlessly rotates. I'm afraid the crowns and faces are going to break away from the base, but it all remains perfectly balanced.

LG: How does that work?

DB: It's a stabile. These all balance on a point.

LG: Do they ever fall off?

DB: They've only ever fallen off when I don't pay attention and the sculptures aren't perpen-

dicular to the bases they're resting on. So if I don't do my job, that's when they fall off. That's the math involved. Like this [he points to a grid with metallic numbers attached to the garden side wall], this is one of Albrecht Durer's magic squares. All of the numbers in each row and column add up to 34.

LG: Would you say your dad was a welder or a mathematician?

DB: Well, he was more than that. Do you know what Girard College is?

LG: I believe it was a school for orphans.

DB: When my dad was a kid...do you remember when you were a kid and there were the tech school girls and guys who, no offense to anybody here, but if you were on the "Home Ec" track or something, you weren't the sharpest tack in the box, so to speak—that was for dummies. Well, at Girard College you had to go to tech classes; my father had a genius I.Q., but he had to go work with his hands. Then he'd wash up and go to math class as part of the requirement. That's what America used to do. People of my father's era were taught these things, how to work with machines, how to take things apart, how to fix things. Whether they used it or not is not the point, just that they had the opportunity to use it. That's who he was.

LG: But he also had an artistic flair.

DB: Yes, on my father's side of the family there

were just a lot of talented people who did things in music and art and whatever, and they were all, like, real smart. So my father was a mathematician for a long time, and he'd built other things as a kid.

LG: What were some of the other things he built?

DB: At Christmastime, my father made me a safe with a combination and everything. It worked, it was big and red with a handle.

LG: Did he put anything inside for you to find?

DB: I'm sure he did, but I can't remember. Right now there's just liquor. He made sets of blocks for my nephews. He always made things, he always built things. He used to do the puppet shows for all of the kids in the neighborhood.

LG: Would he make the puppets himself?

DB: He made all the marionettes, made the stage, and he made me work for him. When I was four years old, I was running the drill press to make an abacus so that he could teach Earnest Evans how to count.

LG: Who's Ernest Evans? [Denis shoots me a look that places me squarely in the 25-45-year-old asshole demographic.]

DB: Chubby Checker. He taught Fabian, he taught all those kids. South Philly, South Philly High. Because Ernest Evans, when the teacher would say something—you ever see him? How big he is? He would just tell the teacher, 'Don't think so,' and go play the piano. He used to come to my house. He loved my old man, he used to bring my parents up on stage at the Forum down in Atlantic City. I mean, he was crazy about him. He went to my sister's prom and told them he was her date. Bishop Egan High School in Levittown, PA—Ernest Evans, aka Chubby Checker, showed up. This is while "The Twist" was out. She was the star for years after that.

LG: So he would tutor kids at his house?

DB: Nope, he taught them in school and they just liked him. My old man, he was like that with people, and I think it comes out in his art, people just liked his art. When I first put these sculptures up, when it was just the hookers, they loved it, they stopped being hookers for the time they stood here and just wanted to talk about the art.

LG: You said the suits and the hookers had similar reactions to the sculptures.

DB: The hookers were just as smart. They would ask the same questions, sometimes better questions. 'How did he make that?' 'What does the sculpture represent?' 'Oh your father made it, what was he thinking when he made it?' The other people were too...whatever to ask those kinds of questions.

LG: They were used to seeing nice things?

DB: No, they just weren't as open as somebody who had nothing. Or less than nothing if that's possible. But...people enjoyed the experience of looking at it. Some fought me at first, they wanted to put down a fucking parking lot here. There's a lot of stuff in my courtyard that I never used. I have enough to go up and down the entire length of fence around the garden.

LG: How long was he making these objects?

DB: Around the time when he retired in the '80's, when I started buying properties in the area. He said, 'Oh this is great, I'm going to retire and we're going to save all our money and not do anything and leave it all to you and your sisters and your brother.' And I'm listening with a typical look on my face and he asks, 'What?' and I say, 'I wouldn't fucking do it for you.' He goes, 'As usual, you're right.' Back then, they had passes that would let you fly anywhere in the U.S. and Canada. I told my parents to buy a couple and they had a blast, they tried everything. They were well-off but frugal.

LG: Which sculptures of his do you plan on bringing out in the future?

DB: I have to install posts and beams and put them up. I just haven't done it yet. I want to put a mural on the wall. I own it. In Philly they're called parting walls, between the rowhouses, so many inches thick. The surface is my half.

LG: You're going to paint it?

DB: No, not me. Arturo Ho is. A friend of mine and my father's, just a wonderful human being. He did a mural in Chinatown. He's just a great person. He's not anything like me. [Laughter.]

LG: Is he part of the Mural Arts program in Philly?

DB: He just did the one in Chinatown. He went and studied with Isaiah [Zagar] on South Street, the one who does all the mirror mosaics. And he was best friends with my dad. For example, they loved to go garage saling and shit. I never liked to go, but Arturo would pick them up at their house in Levittown to go garage saling with them every Saturday. My parents, these Irish folks and this Chinese guy...people would start staring at them and my old man would say stuff like, 'Why are you staring at my son like that?'

LG: What do you think the subject of the mural will be?

DB: I think we're going to do something about my dad. There's some pictures from years ago, before computers were everywhere...he built his first computer, my old man. And he went to the school district and talked them into giving him one of those shorter buses. Then he went to IBM and he told them to give him money and he outfitted the bus with computers and carpeted it and built tables in there, and he would drive it to elementary schools during his free periods. He knew computers would be the way of the future, so he would drive that bus to grammar schools and have the teachers bring the kids out so he could teach them.

LG: So IBM said sure, here are the computers?

DB: Yeah, and here's the money. I think it was just different then, people weren't so fucking greedy for money. People are like animals now. Like with the Main Street Program.

LG: The Main Street Program?

DB: Yes. In the '80's, San Francisco and Philadelphia got grants, the 4500 block at Frankford got a grant. Federal, State and City government put in money. Phase One of many phases was fixing sidewalks, painting the El. I had a few properties in the center of the block. I was living in South America at the time and told my old man to make an art gallery there. He made this beautiful GALLERY @ 1535 sign—which is still there—and beautiful sculptures that went in there, circus wagons with animals for the basement windows and the garden out back. Didn't work out.

LG: And it's not coming back?

DB: Artists are moving in there now. People are bugging me about it being vacant.

LG: Where was his primary workspace? Where was his studio?

DB: In his house. When I was a kid my mother would go out shopping and get food or whatever, and before she'd get back he'd decide to build a giant train platform. So we had doubled the size of our house—we had a living room and a study area and he, well, *we* would start building this platform that took over the study. If you wanted to get in the house you couldn't. My mother'd have to come in the kitchen door. I had my little brother stepping in the plaster—we were making mountains to surround the platform—and then there'd be plaster of paris footprints throughout the house.

LG: Your mother must have been a patient person.

DB: My mother was a saint. She still is.
[He walks back toward Karlie and leads us inside.]

He made the lock on the door. I wanted it to look like a medieval gate but with a modern look to it. I wanted it to have that idea and he came up with it.

LG: Have you seen *Game of Thrones*? I think you'd like it.

DB: I do like that show. He would have liked it. [He points to an intricate stained glass seascape.] He made all this glass.

LG: Did he have favorites? Did he have stretches when he focused on one subject, did he have a first love?

DB: All he wanted to do was whatever crazy shit I would come up with.

LG: You would be the idea man and he would execute.

DB: No, I don't want to take that credit. I would just come up with some off-the-wall bullshit, like, 'Oh, would it be cool if we did this?' and then he would figure it out. He would make the idea better, he would just do more. He built this staircase. He came and measured the hole where the old one used to be. When you build stairs, if you have the rise and the run correct, you almost don't know you're walking on them. You know you're going fucking up, but it's not an effort to walk on. He built full-size models of this in his driveway in Levittown. Nobody could have done this. The math on this is insane. [He sits down at a desk and pulls up a file on his computer.] This'll explain it to you, when I said I would come up with some crazy shit. I would come up with the kernel of the idea, not even, what would you call it...

LG: The germ of the idea?

DB: The amoeba of the fucking idea, ok? I hate even to use the word "idea" because he would figure it all out. So, I used to deal a lot with Japanese arms and armor. The Japanese sword would lay across something called a to kake, a sword stand. I wanted the sword to rest on Sika horns, Japanese deer horns. [He turns to his computer and opens a photo file.] So here's the point: these antlers in the photo are solid silver. I went to my old man and told him that I wanted to make these sword stands, but that I want to make them out of pure silver. Now, to pour something that big and have it come out is virtually impossible because of the flow of the pour. The metal has to be a certain temperature to continue flowing because it's always cooling. It's the lost wax process. [He turns to Amanda.] Artist, come on, a little help here. Chime in.

AG: So, it's not cast. Because you'd have too many pieces.

DB: Well, it is cast, I have all the molds and stuff upstairs. You make the plaster around it, but you have the wax inside. And then you put it in a burn out oven and burn out the wax, and then you're left with the shape. First of all, you have to invent a machine that melts enough silver.

LG: Which he did?

DB: Yes, all of that. They're magnificent. No one...I used to deal a lot in jewelry. And everyone on Jeweler's Row said it couldn't be done. Impossible to do it. All the casters—because I figured I'd go to them first—all the casters said it was totally impossible.

LG: Because of the way the antler is shaped?

DB: No, because of how big it is. 22" high. And how thick it is. And these little points. And you have to get it to pour without any bubbles or any air spaces. The flow has to go down perfectly the whole time from start to finish. You're dealing with something that's like a bazillion degrees and you're pouring it into something else.

25

The flow has to go down perfectly the whole time, from start to finish.

courtesy of DENIS BOYCE

This is the first pour, just one and done. We had fifty-five gallon drums of water there in the shop where he was making it. And he said now we have to wait and we have to do this and we have to do that, and he's telling me, 'I'm not sure it came out, but I can pour it again for you.' And with that—I'm very…well, I'm a little insane, and I just took the whole thing and dropped it into the water so it cooled instantly, and it just exploded, just blew the whole thing out. And I reached in and pulled out two perfect antlers. I said to him, 'I knew they were perfect. I just wanted to show you.' I never liked that my dad would say things like I'm not sure if it worked. I had to show him that they were perfect.

III. Genes and a Piano Player

LG: What did John do after Girard College?

DB: He went into the service, and then he came back and went to LaSalle College, he went to Drexel University...

LG: What did he study there?

DB: Math. Both times. And then he went to Temple for his doctorate.

LG: He basically did a tour of Philadelphia's institutions of higher learning.

DB: He did. He knew everyone around here. George Nakashima. He was a famous wood-worker. Anyway, when I was a kid, he'd heard of my old man and used to invite my mother,

my father and me up to his shop in New Hope. [He pulls up a photo of John George Boyce on the computer bus surrounded by kids.]

LG: I like the bowtie. What's he holding in his hand?

DB: Computers used to have tapes, tape readers. There's the kids, he's showing them about digital tape readers. These are all Digital Equipment Corporation. You do know that Philadelphia was the home of the first computer—Eniac was here at Penn. It was as big as a block, ten million skillion tubes.

LG: That kid he's showing the tape to looks so happy.

DB: That kid is probably driving a Ferrari somewhere now.

LG: When was this taken?

DB: Sometime in the '60's. Look at the fashion, the skirt on the girl. You know, my dad was actually from a well-to-do family. This is part of the story that nobody really knows, but his father, when he married his mother, the guy got disowned and died a month later. They found him in a hotel room in Atlantic City. She was a piano player and a lot more than that...

LG: What was her name?

DB: Her maiden name was Fritz, Dorothy Fritz. I'm named after the Civil War leader, John P. Denney. My father's father's name was John Denney Boyce. When he turned either 18 or 21, he got some inheritance. I don't know why he got it or what it was for. It seems a shame, but that was the convention back then, you married a tart, you got disowned, you married a black person, you got disowned. Then the poor bastard ends up dying in a hotel.

LG: Did you say a couple of months after he got married?

DB: A couple months, yeah. They conceived the kid. My father's father was dead before he was born. Which really is a shame, because he was probably a pretty cool guy. That's probably why my father's so open. This guy married my grandmother, who was a piece of work. My father's father, I'm assuming—the genes are there—that he was an open, giving sort of person.

LG: Because he was willing to give it all up for Dorothy.

DB: He got disowned. How many rich people do you know who'd give up their money? But that's what I'm trying to tell you. Don't just call him a welder. He was more. He was a renaissance man, a mathematician. One of the proudest...he loved that I never had a real job.

LG: Well, you worked. You're working here.

DB: I meant like a job where you work for someone. Working for someone where your boss hollers at you whenever they feel insecure.

LG: That was important to him because you weren't beholden to anyone?

DB: Sort of. My old man had a house and four kids, so it seemed important to him that I had the freedom to do whatever I wanted. Although, he did seem to do whatever he wanted.

After the interview, I walked Amanda home past Heather's gallery and the garden. The signs next to the sculptures are works of metal art themselves and faintly visible in the dusk: "Utah Moon," "A Tree Grows in Brooklyn," "6 Moons over Fishtown," "Honolulu." We stood and looked a little longer, but the sun was setting and there is no artificial lighting in the garden. I heard something shatter and turned to see Heather grabbing a table to move it inside her own shop. Amanda asked if she needed any help.

"It's just a lightbulb," Heather said. "I think the sidewalk can handle it."

C

REVI

PIONE

WHAT SORT OF GIRLS WEAR
LIPSTICK THESE DAYS?

WINT HUSKEY

He left Overland Park, KS early, around 6:30 a.m., but he already knew it would never get told that way because Overland Park could be anywhere and you didn't want your first impression to be a geography lesson. 'I actually drove straight from Kansas City to Philadelphia' was what he would say when he first got there, to Philadelphia. And then pause...allow the audience a moment to guesstimate the enormous distance travelled over...*How long was it?* their astounded faces would ask. '19 hour drive' he would presciently add. 'I just decided to cannonball it.' And smile. They'd like that word—cannonball—ranch parlance maybe? Cheekily verbed-up with a subtle tip of the hat to Burt Reynolds.

Basically, he understood that people *driving* would stop somewhere along the way (Midpoint, Ohio, say) but he wanted the people he'd meet to walk away thinking, 'That guy was on a *run!*' Kansas City and Philadelphia are concrete, far-apart American cities, so you only needed about a fourth-grade education to know that you were dealing with a man who drove across half the country in one night. It sounded impressive and implied that spontaneously exceptional behavior was to be expected.

It was not nice to leave Elizabeth—still busy snoozing—after making promises last night about breakfast. And she knew a place, too. Old friend from college, waking up around noon to an empty so-called guest room. *Dear Liz: Sorry! Didn't want to wake you two up, decided to get an early start, thanks for everything, Ray.* The old adage about omelet-making (inappropriately) came to mind while he stealthily slid into the Alero. His car was the sparkling silver of football helmets and stuffed with liquor store boxes, garbage bags stretched full of soft goods, and bric-a-brac too weirdly-shaped for box or bag (*e.g.*, the ubiquitous acoustic guitar case). Due to the sensitive situation, he had wanted to start the car *softly*, and, knowing what little he did about cars, he turned the key in the ignition like a safe-cracker..."Dammit!" he whispered, swatting at the volume knob in an attempt to silence 93.7's raucous Morning Zoo Crew. What had he been listening to when he got into town last night?! The maladroit whir of the engine caused him to wince, but even the birds were still dozing in the big, quiet trees lining the shady morning street.

He'd never been to a QuikTrip and chose it over the seen-one-seen-'em-all Shell across the street. There was an embarrassing array of coffee canisters to choose from at QuikTrip and a decision was not easily reached as some varieties had descriptively questionable names. What did 'Morning Thunder' do? What was 'Holiday Spice' in observation of (now in late August)?

The cashier was a complete spud, but hidden in the roundness there was something of a spark plug about her. Like how her shift probably began last night but she was still there ringing things up quickly and accurately. "And twenty on three," he said. 'Got it' signaled the long press-ons scuttling over the keypad. Their exchange continued on a dollar-sized screen attached to the register. LG COFFEE REG 1.79, GASOLINE SELF-PUMP 20.00, GRAN BAR CINNA .79, GRAN BAR OATS N' .79. TOTAL 24.31. He grinned but she was now busy invoicing the scene over by the heat-lamped breakfast goods where some day laborers had suddenly amassed. He pushed two bills across the scuffed plexiglass countertop with rolls of scratch tickets curled-up like exotic snakes on display below and got back his change, dimes mostly.

It was morning cool and the sky was weirdly pink, even for a sunrise. *There must be a factory around here somewhere,* he thought. It was tough when pollution made the sky look better. The cicadas were finally quiet, thank god. You'd think everybody was traveling by dirt bike last night. Free to take in the glugging gasoline and thirsty, appreciative sounds of the Alero, he breathed from his mouth and tried to map out his big day of driving. There was not much to consider, though. Here to there was a mostly straight line through what was widely-regarded as not much.

The pump hiccuped and broke his concentration. '*Sale*—$19.64' and directly beneath that '*Gallons*—6.23', like an illustration out of a corny old *Integrated Math I* book.

He returned the nozzle to its tricky holster and drove the car twenty or so feet to a parking space near the entrance. He wasn't cheap, wanting to retrieve more dimes, but some perspective employers had not ruled out the reimbursement of gas and mileage.

* * *

The trip was being made solo. *Less baggage—ha ha—than the last time I moved* (a pun recalling an ex-girlfriend, doubly unfunny). It was finally time to get his story straight. With credits in creative writing from the experimental liberal arts college, he knew that most good stories were the result of a process that, towards the very end, involved considerable editing and deliberative expurgation. So it was convenient that Elizabeth lived in Overland Park, in terms of his *arc*, because he was not eager to explain his early morning flight or the whereabouts of the city itself. But there were bigger holes to address. Being in Philadelphia would be both his a). introduction and e). *denouement*, but b). rising action c). climax, and d). falling action were still hazy. He could see the scribbly notes on his margins: *What happened? (new info. received?); where/how did it come to a head (accept/reject info.?); how does protagonist act on info.? (does s/he gain objective?).*

For the politely inquisitive co-workers and utterly grown-up, there were bold-type vocab terms that they understood and empathized with: *wages, cost of living, job market, career*, and so on. Not an entirely false explanation, although he had not come to his decision after consulting graphs and spreadsheets.

His contemporaries wouldn't need much convincing, of course; they knew well the ignominy of simultaneously holding a degree and serving food.

But mostly he worked on the words reserved for the fleshpots of Philadelphia, the girls who managed to caper through the city in unreasonable heels and low-necked sweaters. Perhaps he would offer a new, fresh take on the dart-sticking-in-the-map bit or, if they appeared too smart for that, merely shrug and offer the defeated-but-not-vanquished look he'd been practicing in the rearview mirror. There was a real story behind that last contrivance, which lent it believability, but it was still open-ended and he could never tell it right.

* * *

The "Show Me State" was as wildly green and sunny and pastoral as land near an interstate highway can be. Based on road trips with guitars he and his friends called 'tours', he knew Missouri would be beautiful at the end of summer. The leaves always seemed too healthy and plentiful for it to be any other way. Four crows picked at something daringly close to traffic. *Murder. Roadkill*, he thought, but that was soon behind him and the trees were back to being, as instructional painter Bob Ross would say, happy.

The black Range Rover didn't make any noise when it charged from his left and suddenly appeared in front of him, narrowly avoiding the emerald Taurus in the far lane. A truly foreign vehicle. He reflexively jerked the wheel about two degrees and a few mugs loudly clanked together in backseat recognition of such canny restraint.

"Jesus jumped up bald-headed Christ!" he yelled, which helped to defuse the lingering fear.

He'd have to work on his swearing if he was going to make it on the East Coast. The Rover sped ahead with a vanity plate like a big middle finger pointed right back at him: we were now dealing with BIGMAC2.

"Learn to drive, BIGMAC2, you fat, cheesy bitch."

It was a start. He assumed that the plate was in reference to the iconic cheeseburger (which meant, in turn, that the driver must've been a tub). You didn't see Range Rovers in the drive-thru, though. Could that car even make it *through* the drive-thru? Would the owner of an imposing status symbol actually *go in to* a McDonald's? And dine-in? Filling up little paper cups with ketchup and fetching her own fountain drink? Nothing was as it seemed. With his right thumb he upped the cruise control, keeping the Alero within sight of his new bête noir until he reached uncomfortable speeds.

*　*　*

It was still early in the day when he saw the Arch not far from where Mark McGuire smacked so many dingers. It was so colossally impressive in person! He switched off a local dealership's otherwise appealing offer of *free bonus cash* in order to focus better. Pictures never could properly invoke this. Such daring *heft!* The handiwork of what must have been some radical school of non-Euclidian architecture got him thinking: was he betraying his hearty pioneer stock by heading eastward right under the *Gateway to the West*? His predecessors had put in long hours making the whole western United States livable and now he was ungratefully retreating to, of all places, *Philadelphia*. They were surely rotating (slow, rotisserie-style) in rocky frontier graves.

For a few days he had been able to convince himself that he was something of a pioneer, a *re-settler*. His 'ins' out there had even told him that the natives were backwards and hostile towards new things and ideas...*Hm. Explorer or scavenger, intrepid or opportunistic? Discuss.* Growing up in Idaho (a place where, according to lore, every sign of progress had once been a pasture), you always blamed it on Californians: bad driving, Mexican people, all these damned *cafes*, and so on. The circumstances were different...but...not.

Back to the Arch, though (it's visible from a distance, so he had time to think): somehow there was an elevator inside the monument that takes visitors to a sort of panopticon set in the middle of the great curve. It's what people *would* write home about: *Hi from the Gateway Arch! Having a good time. Saw stadiums, old buildings, and those pretzel-y freeway knots. Must admit, very cool! You should definately [sic.] visit it someday. Tell Dad, Sheila, and Gram I say "Hi." Love,*

Kevin. He wanted to be inside the Arch, too, and figured that beating his own postcard to Philadelphia would be a perfectly jaunty thing to do, but the diversion wasn't as fun as it seemed and would involve getting off the freeway, parking ($$), paying to get into the Arch/riding the elevator ($$$), buying a postcard and stamp ($)...

Just across the river was East St. Louis, which he'd read about and seminared on in coursework exploring inequity and social justice issues. Driving through it, he saw grime like never before and gassed up a few exits later in Collinsville.

Too scared to pull over here, but you're moving to Philly? a little goblin-y voice said inside.

* * *

Illinois, down near the bottom where rivers meet, was, and presumably *is*, quiet. The green here was tame and regular. Judging by the signs along the road, this country was all gas, food, and lodging.

The more confrontational, usually homemade signs reminded him of Amy, who had been pregnant for five or six weeks that past winter in Albuquerque. She announced it just as he was about to get out of bed and make the morning's coffee.

"Honey," she said, "I'm pregnant." She smiled sheepishly until she got visual confirmation that he was smiling and very soon everybody was happy and smiling.

"So-oo...can you do caffeine?" he asked once it all settled in.

He was proud of how he kept composed, never crying or even thinking his life was over. It naturally happened when they least wanted it and, still, he felt prepared to make it work like so many people had done throughout history. Together they suffered in that softer meaning of the word and adjusted schedules and routines accordingly. They hadn't opted out of the pregnancy; it just didn't happen. There was no saying for sure how she took all of this. And he couldn't imagine it now anyway (the swollen belly, the semi-Mormon lifestyle), not after the way *he* left town. Today was about what was to be, not what might have been. Everything had already decided against what might have been.

* * *

The radio kept decent company for some stretches, but it usually ended up being Tom Petty and whatever happened to be popular at the time. He wanted to catch a low-frequency sermon preaching kooky stuff over the airwaves, somebody manically shouting, "Christ is your pit crew chief!" at him. Authors were always slipping these sorts of one-liners into their characters' long journeys across the country. He couldn't find anything, though. The religious stations may have wised up. Every inch of the dial (so to speak, his car was an '04 and had a digital tuner) let him down. A smart British voice was detailing *new* strife in war-ravaged Africa. Country music sure didn't sound 'like it used to.' Neither did rap, apparently. "At least Tom Petty's cool," he said as "American Girl" came on, guns blazing.

* * *

Drive Hammered/Get Nailed/DUI Enforcement In Effect the safety-orange-colored road sign flashed. Indiana welcomes you! It was 1:30 p.m. and he was feeling that coffee. He was a shaky, cranky caricature of the overly-caffeinated. He had no patience for the agitated radio evangelist that showed up too late. "*Pokemon* world is a world of the devil, of the Satanic...You might not take it seriously, but I assure you *Satan* takes it quite seriously. *Demons* take it quite seriously." It turned out to be not that fun. Elizabeth had called again but still didn't leave a message. He no longer cared and, in fact, didn't give so much as a *rat's* ass. No telling if this was a blood sugar thing or his true disposition surfacing, ugly and gatorlike. Morale had dipped. His thinking was already turning *unsound*.

At a Flying J outside of a town named Brazil, he peeled crinkling Saran off a $4.49 submarine sandwich and cast the roast beef off for whatever parking lot fauna would have it (for what fool would scarf Flying J lunch meat with so many miles to go?). He should have known that the days of seasonally-rotated pies and ever-fresh coffee were as anachronistic as the nickle such fare would cost you in the make-believe diner. The sun was out and bright. The various receipts on his person were absorbing a now ever-present moisture. Small dogs were shitting in the gravel and yapping, the result of hundreds of years of carefully-monitored husbandry. A plane was slowly making its way across the sky and a sticky wad of underchewed bread stuck to the roof of his mouth, just out of tongue's reach. *Nothing's ever easy*, he thought.

A middle-aged blonde woman was speaking frantically into a cell phone she appeared to be shoving into the side of her face. She and her son were going back to Gary. Did she mean the town or the man? It could be both. Either Gary sounded tough. Through it all, her son (ten or eleven by the looks of it) was launching a hacky sack straight up in the air and trying to catch it.

He had made a game of it and announced a score of 13-to-8.

Mom held the phone to her ear and watched the boy. She wore a *Jesus, did anybody even care?* expression.

"Cody, quit throwin' that thing around the cars!"

"It's soft," he explained before losing it in the sun.

"Well you're gonna lose the damn thing, then. No, not you," she explained to her listener. "I was talking to Cody."

The hacky sack hit the ground a few feet to his left and he urgently ran over and scooped it up. "13-to-*10*."

The sandwich lasted only a few wolfish bites. He no longer gave a rat's ass about the new people, still twelve hours away, excited to hear his story and ready to be won over by his oodles of charm...*right*. What story? He knew he had no charm then and that it would take days to recover, probably.

Beneath the hood the engine still crackled and clicked so he gave it a deserved rest. Tony's 'guy' back in Albuquerque had told him to do this after giving the Alero a tune-up. "Don't drive around for ten hours straight or nothing." It was the only advice he could remember. A few more minutes would do.

A light breeze refreshed without the taint of diesel—just good, country air. Everything here was on the top of a small hill, probably the result of the nearby on-ramp and exit. You could look down and see houses, all single-storied and made of yellowish bricks. Lush, irrigated lawns. Simple and well-spaced, like where his great-grandparents had lived.

If you really wanted to start over, this is the kind of place you'd move to, he thought, the "you" impersonal, hypothetical. *This is, after all, the kind of place that Witness Protection sends people to. There* was something interesting: bureaucrats in Virginia offices brokering deals for inconspicuous real estate two time zones west, covertly setting up phony employment ('*Don't worry, you'll get the hang of it*', a knowing wink), faxing a fictionalized family history memorandum...

* * *

There was no congestion on the roads but thoughts of 'making good time' were cynically tamped down. He held frequent apostrophic pep talks, lectures, and heart-to-hearts in the Alero, particularly with Amy. All through Ohio he spoke to and thought of her. Eight hours of driving had broken him (in interrogative jargon), and he allowed himself to admit that, yes, Amy Burns was a factor in his decision to move.

She was from Cleveland and liked to go back for visits often. Amy was so mid-western it pained him. Not far underneath the tattoos and behind the pierced septum was a very nice girl who wouldn't even call it 'sex'—they 'made out' instead. "So pretty. Never *had to* wear make-up. She loved gingham and polka dots, but she never went all-out nostalgia or anything. Never walked around with a bouffant and a pie." Her hair was modern and self-cut but, wait, *didn't she really like pie?* he wondered, *Was that one of her things?*

He pulled over to call from the rest stop-cum-welcome center when he first entered the state, but thankfully nobody answered. *Who knows what I would have said!* he concluded after going over, in detail, the various ways the conversation might have unfolded. Like a *Choose Your Own Adventure* book, many of his decisions resulted in speculative misfortune. But what he had said (to the answering machine (because Amy was the only person in the developed world still relying on a landline and answering machine (and hard-to-find tiny cassettes))) was: "Hi, it's Ray. I'm in Ohio. Wanted to say 'Hi.'...Guess you're not home, though. Obviously. So-oo. I'll talk to you later... O.K. Bye."

He was not normally so halting in his delivery, but he wanted to give her time to pick up. It was well-established that she never answered the phone without hearing who it was first, anyway— she claimed an irrational fear that her Uncle Jack might be on the other end, and she never had the heart to cut his long-winded, wandering conversations short. Of course, he saw through all of that. She did this to obtain leverage in discussions: talking on *her* terms. He'd seen her do it, letting honest people obliviously chatter while she did not deign to respond. Even if his live audience was only the doughy orange cat she kept, he still had succeeded in planting the information. Eventually she would hear that he was in her beloved Ohio, which would sting twice (he had never claimed to be a gracious loser).

He gave himself the *You look like shit* look in the rearview mirror near dusk and West Virginia; both car and driver needed a break. An enormous, faded fiberglass hamburger was planted next to a service station that was clearly too small to contain a grill. Another riddle of the ancients: who put it there and what became of them? The building was small and square, with wood siding stained a shade darker than the radioactive beef patty in the yard. The roof could use some sprucing up. There was a reddish picnic table off to the side, badly splitting and waterlogged, and a reticent reader board that said 'Open'. He eased into third pump's minute domain and killed the engine. The Alero wheezed and sputtered while he sat still for a moment and listened with a solemn, clinical air. If the car had a tongue, like in some of the recent popular animated features, it would be comically poking out to one side of its grill/mouth. Maybe he should just stay there, wherever he was, and make folk art. Do studies of the burger. He could boldly paint flat and bright pictures. Anything but more driving.

Sucking in a breath and undoing the seat belt, he swung the door open and lurched out into the bug-loud glade. The great plains were not-so-suddenly at his arrears. Elevation. Portents of mountains. He filled 'er up and went inside to pay.

A nice bookend to the now well-forgotten start of the day (although his destination was far away still), he went inside and got another large coffee, some snacks, and twenty dollars on three. He needed to talk to a kind person while he was still in Ohio. It was like the signs in the desert warning travelers about the vast distance between facilities, only this time it was a final shot at nice.

"I'm driving to Philadelphia," he said to the turkey-shaped cashier.

"Philadelphia?"

"City of Brotherly Love."

Neither moved. Was he supposed to explain why to her?

"Hm. That's not what I hear, honey."

Honey! That was nice. She was being so nice. And he looked so haggard and had started to smell.

"Nah, I've got some friends out there."

"Oh, well, that's better. You be good now."

He smiled, demonstrating his obedience to her right there in the store.

Oh boy, he thought. He was going to end up like Balzac, who died from drinking so much coffee that his heart exploded or gave out, he forgot which. The prolific man would write and write, guzzling coffee non-stop. It being a newer drink at the time, nobody thought to recommend that he cut back. Meanwhile: A big, beat-up truck exuded character across the gravel lot. There was a solitary figure inside, pinching the last of his fries and dropping them into his mouth. *You seldom* see *happy people eating fast food alone*, he thought while cleverly using the plastic packaging to sluice cheese-and-peanut butter cracker crumbs into his mouth. He savored the orange array of flavor. *Feelings of compromise and regret on the horizon, as close and visible as any hood ornament. This is the norm for this dude, presumably named Norm.* The rust-calico Dodge Ramcharger Prospector 4x4 had wheel wells that vanished before onlookers' eyes because of how they salted roads here. The driver and his 'nother day/'nother dollar' mien crept up to the road and turned left towards what looked like town.

* * *

It was hard to feel weepy sitting next to such a big hamburger, so once he was back on the road the truck and the dude immediately reminded him of the saddest story he knew. Amy's face would change when she mentioned her dad, even just in passing. You might think he was still alive, the way her voice brightened up and how subtly she modified tenses. His jumping off a bridge was one of the first things she'd mentioned when they met, though. And it wasn't an *I'm fucked up, let's just be honest* first date sort of introduction...it was while he was a trainee at their shared workplace. When he did get closer to her and learned about her dad's job at the (no lie) *clothes hanger factory* (making the twisty metal kind (with their strong ties to illicit abortion, *Mommie Dearest*, and closeted moments of frustration)), in Cleveland, Ohio, for years (decades?) on the night shift before, well...it was not so long ago, when she and her sister were both safe and college-aged and independent. Springsteen without a melody or a hook. Just a very sad and real story that took place in the USA.

Now there was the grim association between all of this and the up-and-coming neighborhood he was moving to and the room in the "Factory Loft" he would rent in Philadelphia. People were clearly drawn to the idea that they might live where bow ties or candy used to be made, but have they considered the mauled fingers? The horrific taffy scaldings? It was like Scatman Crothers warned in *The Shining* about the lingering smell of burnt toast. Sure, the working man had no country (especially in today's economy), but that didn't mean you were granted access to the industrial zone. That factory loft was recently a defunct eyesore of the mutton-chopped tycoon times, but not everyone thought spacious and contemporary were necessarily preferable. There was discord over unsightly solar panels and raised backyard garden beds, even. And while he worried about his *bon mots* and mooned over his own glorious initiative, some would hear ugly vowels and see a stupidly stolid 'tude. *Here comes the jackass, prying open the ossuary doors and ready for his nap...*

Even Burt Reynolds had a passenger, some comic relief, somebody to take the wheel during the boring parts. 6:30 a.m. was so long ago now. He needed a rest.

* * *

One time, the summer before, while camping with friends at Chaco Canyon, he'd heard one of the burn-out millionaires from Taos ask a park ranger what kind of drugs the people there had been on. "Spiritually speaking, of course," he added.

"Well," the ranger replied, "the scant records we have indicate that they *didn't* partake in any of the readily-available psychoactives, though they knew of them. Instead, those wishing to attain some sort of," he turned to the burn-out, "*spiritual awakening* would go off into the desert away from the great houses and dance for days without stopping."

That about describes the rest of the drive east towards the sunrise. It was very dark out by then and there were few functioning parts of his brain outside the more basic portions surrounding the stem. He had a certain mad dog look in his eyes that unsettled even the toll plaza veterans. He crossed the Delaware the wrong way and had to pay five bucks to get another crack at it then wandered derelict through an empty Chinatown where strange roots and vegetables were carted off of idling trucks. But he ultimately got there, closer to twenty hours' drive.

* * *

For the most part people welcomed him. Few people in Philadelphia had heard of *Cannonball Run* and the sheetrock walls of his room betrayed much of the mystique he'd hoped to cultivate. Somebody broke the backseat window of his car and stole a sack of *Scrabble* tiles, but that wasn't an act of hostility aimed at a vehicle with New Mexico tags. It was just another desperate person, the kind whose pleading and recriminations he already tuned out automatically.

Sometimes you would find him at the bar, drinking a tall can of inexpensive beer. The unwitting president of the Club That Would Have Him For A Member all over again!

"So why did you move from Albuquerque?" She had crazy, intense Manson family eyes and a matching outfit. "I heard it was so beautiful out there."

"You're thinking of Santa Fe," he leisurely replied before tipping the beer can back. There's no face, no look, besides the placid one that a tall beer imparts around this time of the evening, after work. "I was just ready to leave, I guess," which is the truest answer he could ever give.

"I'm pretty sure my friend lived in Albuquerque." She pursed her mouth in the style of a perplexed six-year-old cutie pie for a moment. Then came a very earnest, almost disgusted face. "Do you have a girlfriend?" She wanted to sound *cross*.

"No," he said—also true and to-the-point—"no girlfriend, no missus." But she was just asking and is right back to winsome face-scrunching and suggestively thigh-stroking. "Just you and me." *I already don't remember her name.* He knew she would demand he repeat it to her once they were intimately tangled but still partially clothed. "Where are you from?" he asked, looking at the smudged rim of her vodka tonic, innocently wondering what sort of girls wear lipstick these days.

CARS WITHOUT HUBCAPS
John Aylesworth

...leave Wal Mart, start out Route 50
toward rusty double-wides and farms
left to forest, places where crossroads
had names once, stops on trails west.
Old Chevys and Fords with wrinkles
rattle away, leaving town for homesteads
tucked under hills claimed by pioneers
manifesting destiny, without engines.
What's left is mud and gravel,
and folks with only names to cling to,
legacies lost when the four lane
cut through the valley, made tradition
and birthright as bleak as cars without hubcaps.

Covered wagon with jackrabbit mules encounters an automobile on the trail near Big Springs, Nebraska
A. L. Westgard, 1912 | National Archives and Records Administration

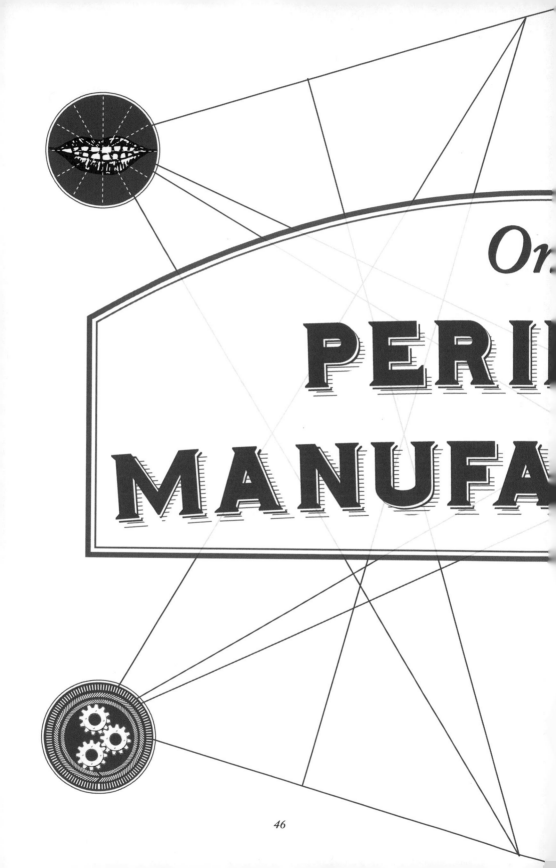

On

PERI

MANUFA

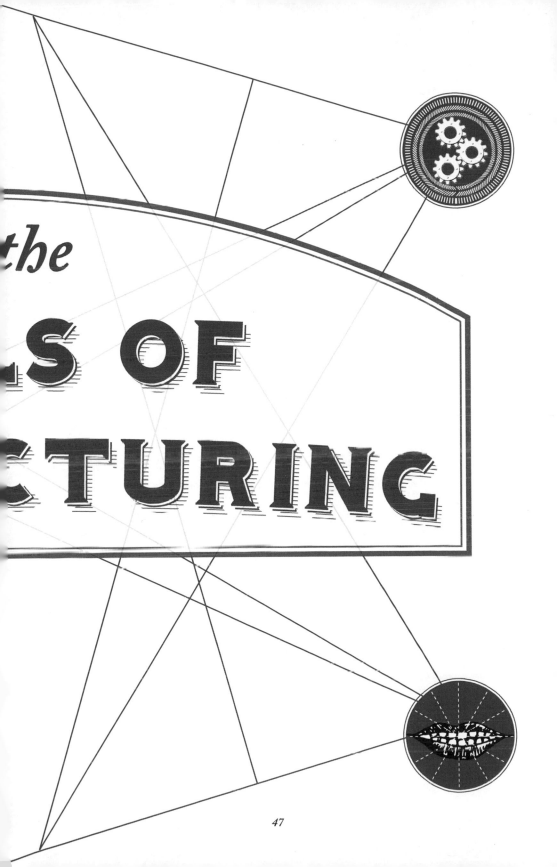

the

S OF

CTURING

RADIUM GIRLS

LIZ KERR

It wasn't until young girls started turning up dead, until the media had tagged the killer with a catchy name, that people began to show any concern. Even her ex, to whom she hadn't spoken in a good six, maybe seven months, checked in.

"I heard about this Kensington Strangler," he said, "you being careful?"

"I'm fine. He's targeting the prostitutes on the Avenue."

"I told you not to move down there. Watch out for those Kenzos, Veronica."

She didn't know how to answer that because, by birthright, she was a Kenzo, too.

Every big city has a neighborhood that provides fodder for the stand-up acts of local comedians, an inside joke enjoyed by the more well-off citizenry. London has the East End, Boston has Southie. In Philadelphia, it's Kensington and its denizens, known as Kenzos.

Veronica had spent the first two years of her life in Kensington. Her father worked in an aluminum window frame factory, but in the late '70's the owners scabbed out to a new plant in a non-union state down South. The once booming factories and textile mills that had kept the neighborhood flush for a century had nearly all been shuttered. Her grandmother, who had worked for thirty years in the cutting room of the great Stetson Hats Company, still blamed J.F.K. for his decision to go hatless in his inaugural parade.

"After that photo of him on the front page, none of the men wanted to wear hats anymore."

Like dust bowl families in search of work, her parents joined the migrating tide of families who packed up and moved out of Kensington. Her father found work in the Fairless Hills Steel Mill, just north of the city, and they moved into a bungalow a few blocks from the main gate. He was hired as a scarfer, the dirtiest, most dangerous job in the mill. Wearing a fireproof suit and mask and armed with a blowtorch, he inspected the hot slabs of steel that rolled out of the blast furnace. Any visible defects would be burnt off with a blast from his torch.

On summer nights when it was too hot to sleep, Veronica would fold her pillow against the window ledge and watch the night sky shimmer in a reddish orange haze as vapor poured from the mill's massive chimney. Sometimes on a Saturday night, her parents and neighbors—the scarfers and smelters and cindermen and their wives—would set out folding chairs in a circle on the tiny front lawn. The ebb and flow of their conversation, the low, soft laughter of parents whose children were in bed, would drift up to her window. She liked this view of their true selves, unposed.

Her family would return to Kensington on Sundays and holidays to visit her grandmother. As they drove through the neighborhood her parents would point out all that had disappeared—stores and gas stations and neighbors. It seemed to Veronica the only things left were churches and bars and the former didn't get nearly as much business as the latter. Her parents tried to convince her grandmother to move in with them, but she was proud of her tiny row home.

On afternoons when the adults would play cards at the dining room table, Veronica would lie on the floor and flip through her grandmother's photo albums, looking for herself in the faces of long gone relatives. One day she discovered an old newspaper wrapped in tissue paper buried at the bottom of the album box. Veronica unfolded it. It was dated 1932.

"Who're these girls?" Veronica asked and pointed to a front page photo with the caption *Doomed Radium Girls.* The photo was taken inside a factory and showed a long table with a row of young women holding paint brushes.

The adults put down their cards. Her grandmother gently laid the newspaper on the table. "This one," she pointed out one of the women, "is your great-grandmother."

"What are they painting?" Veronica asked, but her grandmother was staring at the photo and didn't answer.

"They're painting the numbers on the dials of watches," her mother answered, "so they'll glow in the dark."

"The brushes would lose their shape, so they were told to make a point with their lips," her grandmother said. "I remember my mother would tuck me in and turn out the light and her mouth would glow in the dark."

When Veronica was in high school, she did a history project on the Radium Girls and realized why her grandmother didn't talk much about what had happened to her mother. The factory owner had paid a doctor to report that the women's symptoms—bleeding, anemia, and tumors of the mouth and jaw—were from syphilis.

In her junior year, the Fairless Hill Steel Mill closed down due to competition from cheaper, imported steel. Veronica took a part-time job at Sesame Place (a Disney-fied version of Sesame Street) to help with the bills. Initially, she was hired as a "walker." She would walk through the park dressed as Big Bird, waving and posing for photos with children, but she soon grew tired of the heat, the headpiece, and the little boys with a penchant for punching characters in the privates.

When the position of photographer's assistant was posted on the staff room bulletin board, she applied immediately. Technically, the position was photographer's cashier, but the studio was air-conditioned so she made the switch. Parents would line up with their children for a picture with Cookie Monster, like Santa at the mall, and Veronica would sell them the photo package—wallet size, 5x7, or 8x10. The photographer was Mrs. Egan, the Visual Arts teacher from her high school, and on rainy days when the studio traffic was slow, she taught Veronica about cameras, composition, and lighting. Eventually, Veronica became confident enough in her own skill to ask if she could shoot a few of the customers, and Mrs. Egan agreed she was ready.

She oriented to the view from behind the lens and discovered that, by developing the negative, she could see the image more clearly. After high school, her family's financial situation ruled out attending a four-year college, but she felt it was a waste of her time anyway. She booked assignments for the weddings, Bar Mitzvahs, and First Communions of friends and family. In a few short years, she had become self-sufficient. And bored. The sight of middle-aged women snap dancing to "Celebrate Good Times" made her want to smash her light kit.

On days when she had no paid assignments, she would drive down to Kensington to shoot freelance from the street. She shot in black and white film that, unlike digital, allowed for infinite shades of gray. A series of photos she did on abandoned factories that she titled "Scabbed" won a Best in Show at a juried photographic exhibit. One of the judges commented, "These images celebrate Philadelphia's past in the way Romans venerate the crumbling aqueducts."

Her ex didn't understand the pull of the city. "If you're searching for your roots, there's those ancestry apps for that. You don't have to be down there walking the streets of Kensington." She gradually stopped telling him about where she went and what she shot. She stopped telling him much of anything.

* * *

Early one January morning she pulled her car to the side of the road let the engine idle, savoring a few more moments of warmth and quiet before making her approach. She'd noticed the construction crew a few days earlier and made a note to come back at an hour when she wouldn't have to dodge pedestrians while working. Most of the crews in the neighborhood were demolition, so this reversal of physical effort felt oddly refreshing. On the job site stood an empty, ten-story brick textile mill. The men sat on top of Igloo coolers and upended work buckets, eating breakfast sandwiches and nursing coffee cups in the cold.

She started shooting from across the street and then moved in closer. One of the men called out to her.

"Is that for GQ?" He started mugging and the other guys laughed.

Veronica laughed, too. "Not GQ, no. It's a freelance project."

"You want some coffee, hon?" the funny one, probably the foreman, asked.

"Oh, no thank you. I'm good. What are you guys working on?"

"Officially, it's gonna be called the Kensington Arts House."

"An art school?"

"No, housing for, like, artsy types. It's got the funding trifecta behind it—federal, state and city."

"No shit." She took a few more shots and accepted their second offer of hot coffee.

***

Veronica kept her coat on as she searched for the Kensington Arts House website later that afternoon, unable to fully thaw after the session at the job site. The project was modeled after New Deal ventures of the 1930's that used artists to help revitalize poverty-stricken areas. The mill would be converted into twenty-eight rent-controlled apartments with the first two floors dedicated to common shared space—painter's studios, sound-proof rehearsal rooms, a gallery space, and a darkroom. Veronica completed her residency application that night.

***

Later that month she was summoned for an interview with the selection board. She walked through the double doors of the office clutching the paperwork she had been asked to bring, including her last three tax returns, her current bank statement, and her portfolio. The three members of the board, appointees of the Mayor's Commission on the Arts, asked her to speak about her artistic goals.

Veronica wished she had prepared more thoroughly for the interview. She had hoped her portfolio would speak for her. Public speaking, even to a small audience, made her feel nervous and overexposed. Her cheeks burned as she began to ramble about smokestacks and shadows, beaming Bar Mitzvah boys, her grandmother's faded newspaper, and the clarity of negatives.

"I'm so sorry," she said. "What was the question again?"

"What are your artistic goals?"

By way of further explanation, she could only think to ask them a question. "Did you ever see the photo "Migrant Mother"?"

"The dust bowl woman?" one of them asked.

Veronica nodded. She thought, *If we sat here all day, I still wouldn't be able to put it into words.*

***

The official notice of acceptance came as a certified letter. The tentative move-in date was ten months away. It actually took closer to a year, but Veronica didn't mind. She did a time lapse series of photos on the renovation and displayed it at the ribbon-cutting. She took a group photo of the construction gang and gave each of the guys a copy.

***

Girl #1 was found in a weed-strewn lot off the Avenue the week Veronica moved in to the Arts House. Initially, her death was assumed to be a drug overdose, an all too common event in the neighborhood. When the autopsy revealed that the cause of death was strangulation, little attention was paid.

Veronica met the other inhabitants of her building at a resident's meeting in the first floor common area. Of the twenty-eight apartments, eight were claimed by painters, five by actors, four by filmmakers, four by musicians, three by writers, two by sculptors, and one by a fellow photographer. They worked out a system for sharing studio time, rehearsal stages, and the dark room. They posted sign-up sheets for a monthly showcase of work in the first floor gallery. They planned First Friday events, shared cell numbers, and friended each other on Facebook.

In the morning, she broke down her cardboard moving boxes and carried them out to the recycling dumpster in the parking lot behind the building. At first she thought the rustling sound might be one of the feral cats that prowled the area. She peeked behind the dumpster and saw a girl sitting on the ground, bent over and tapping at her bare foot. Her long, stringy hair was dyed a dull, yellowish blond color with a good inch of brown roots showing.

"Oh, sorry," Veronica said, and the girl looked up. She was holding a syringe between her lips. Veronica took a step back as the girl, in a swift motion, injected the syringe into the top of her foot. "Oh," Veronica said again and quickly went back inside the Arts House and up to her apartment.

It wasn't the first time she'd seen someone shooting up, but this girl looked so young and fragile and defenseless. *What if she stops breathing and needs CPR?* Veronica thought, *What if she vomits and chokes or one of the neighborhood pit bulls that no one seems to own comes upon her?* She grabbed her cell, ran down the steps and back out to the dumpster. The girl was gone. Veronica went around to the front of the building and saw her walking slowly toward the avenue. She tried to catch up to her, but a car pulled over and the girl got in.

That afternoon, Veronica set up her equipment in the studio to do head shots for the actors in an upcoming production of *Hamlet*, taking particular care with her lighting of Karlie, the actress with almost translucent skin playing Ophelia. Karlie chatted with Veronica between shots and offered her tickets to their opening night performance. Veronica told Karlie about the morning encounter behind the building, but she didn't seem surprised.

"Get used to it," Karlie told her, "they're called Kenzos."

+++

Veronica sipped a coffee in the Dunkin Donuts on the Avenue until the afternoon light began to fade. As the street lights came on, the prostitutes took up their posts, leaning against the rusting iron beams that held up the elevated train, framed like women in the windows of Amsterdam's red light district. The El train covered the street like a lid over a box, blocking out the stars and bathing the women in a phosphorescent glow of street lamps mixed with headlights. Veronica worked both sides of the road, moving quickly back and forth, searching for the next shot.

"You need to offer people cigarettes," a girl said, half-concealed behind a pillar, "if you want them to pose."

Veronica looked closely. It was the girl from the dumpster. It might have been the effect of the shadows, but she seemed older than she had in the morning light, possibly early twenties. "I don't want posed," Veronica said, "I want natural."

"This ain't natural, that's for damn sure."

"Sorry, I didn't mean that. Is it okay if I photograph you?"

The girl lit a cigarette, nodded her approval, and leaned out into the street as if waiting on a taxi. "You live in that artists' house," she said.

"I'm Veronica." She lifted her camera and began shooting.

"April," she answered, and popped her jaw to form a perfect smoke ring that Veronica captured as it haloed above her head. Aside from the occasional El train passing overhead and the clicking of the mirror/shutter mechanism in her camera, they worked in silence until a man in a mini-van pulled alongside Veronica.

"You working?" he asked.

April quickly stepped up to his window. "I am. You looking for a date?" He nodded and she got in the passenger side without looking back.

***

When the Medical Examiner confirmed that a second girl, found in a vacant lot not far from the first, had been strangled in the same manner, more attention was paid. The DNA match generated talk of a serial killer and the media declared him the Kensington Strangler.

An emergency meeting for all Arts House residents was called. It was led by one of the sculptors. "I'm sure you've all been getting panicky calls from your friends and family," she said. "We have to look at ways to protect ourselves."

There was excited talk of mace, the buddy system, and heightened security.

"What about the girls on the Avenue?" Veronica asked. No one had any suggestions.

***

She spent the next Saturday back in Fairless Hills, shooting a wedding with a Victorian theme. When she returned to the Arts House, news trucks were parked up and down the Avenue, local and major networks this time. She reached into her purse and realized she had turned off her phone in the church. She had five missed calls. The first three were her mother: "Veronica, come home, there's a Jack the Ripper down there!" The next was from one of the actors: "Another woman was found. Call me when you get close, I'll walk you from the parking lot."

The last was from her ex. She pressed delete.

Everyone had gathered around a TV in the common room. There was a third confirmed victim. She'd been found along the railroad tracks behind the Arts House. The Guardian Angels were patrolling the area along with extra police. A tipster hotline was set up and another zero had been tacked on to the reward. A police sketch of the suspect filled the screen. Veronica studied it, but it was vague and his head was covered by a hoodie. She held up her hands to focus on the face alone, but she didn't recognize him.

The next morning detectives interviewed the inhabitants of the Arts House. They asked if any-one had noticed anything, had seen a person who fit the suspect's description or if they had shot any video or photos in the area recently. Veronica told them she had and that if they came back in the afternoon she would have the shots developed. She asked the detectives if they knew the third victim's name, but they said they were still looking for her family and couldn't reveal it.

Veronica took the roll of film marked "April" into the dark room. She set up three trays and mixed the chemicals for each: developer, stop bath, and fix. First, she pressed the negative to the photo paper and dropped it into the developer tray. She gently agitated the paper, rocking it back and forth until April's features appeared, glowing in the chemicals. She gently lifted the image with a pair of tongs and washed it in the stop bath until finally dropping it in the fix tray. Under the solution April appeared to be drowning, pulled down by the water, incapable of her own distress.

RADIATOR HEAT

CHRISTOPHER WINK

It was very strange for Reginald to be back.

Not like walking into your childhood bedroom for the first time in years and it looking the exact same, but like walking into your childhood bedroom for the first time in years and finding someone had built a row of modern, high-priced townhouses in the middle of it.

"This block of Almond Street was always a good one," said Reginald, riding in the passenger seat alongside the square-jawed real estate agent who was parking the car.

"Exactly," said the agent. "And this property is completely renovated: central air, two updated bathrooms, remodeled kitchen and ceiling fans throughout."

"Ceiling fans?" said Reginald without much thought.

The pair walked to the house, cars neatly parked on either side of the one way street. The tightly packed red brick row homes were interrupted by a stucco front here and a faux stone front there.

"Yes, Reginald. Ceiling fans," said the real estate agent with the seriousness of a priest in confession.

"All these homes used to have that shiny silver aluminum window framing," said Reginald, glancing up and down the street. "It's how you knew you were in the neighborhood."

"Oh, yes," said the agent. "Fortunately, you don't much see it anymore, most of it's been taken down. People finally came to their senses, I guess. Wood is back in now, really helps resale value."

The neighborhood your grandfather found in the beginning of the 20th century is the one your father ran away from and the one you're currently seeking an investment property in. Reginald never remembered any ceiling fans when his father would drive him into the neighborhood to visit his grandfather.

"This place has been practically entirely gutted," gushed the agent as he fumbled through a collection of keys. "New windows, doors, sheetrock in most rooms. It still has the old radiator heat though."

"Good," said Reginald with great purpose.

UPON RIPPING HIS NOTES TO SHREDS, CHARLES SCHWAB SPEAKS

(from a speech given on New Year's Day, 1930)

Jackie Campbell

I want to speak to you
from the heart, to tell you
my own personal thoughts.

I want to glory and rejoice
in the opportunity
to expand,

to hear men talk
about America's situation today.
What do you want me to do?

Carnegie wrote:
It will be a great mistake
for the community

to shoot the millionaires,
for they are the bees
that make the most honey.

I disagreed with his ideas
on how to best distribute the wealth.
I spent mine!

Rejoice and expand!
Compared to what this country will be,
we haven't even reached the foothills.

O, glory and rejoice
as though we had reached
the summit.

I hear men talk in despair.
What do you want me to do?
Cause a panic?

Or.

ANATO
COAL
POWER

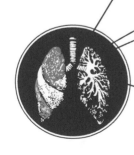

the

MY OF A

FIRED

PLANT

UNDER THIS CLOUD

LIFE AND DEATH IN THE SHADOW OF
A COAL-FIRED POWER PLANT

SARAH GREY

The birthplace of environmentalist Rachel Carson, her homestead is open to the public...We are proud to call ourselves the town "where green was born."

—*SpringdaleBorough.com*

In the end, Rachel Carson remembered only how embarrassed she was by...how dreary and dirty the working-class town became when the West Penn Power Company and Duquesne Light Company squeezed it between their huge power stations at both ends, and how endlessly ugly Springdale was.

—Linda Lear, *Rachel Carson*

My friends who aren't from the Rust Belt think it's weird that I grew up playing in industrial waste, but my friends from home understand.

We grew up in the shadow of the Duquesne Light smokestack, the brown one with red and white stripes. (It's called GenOn Energy now, a name meant to sound clean—to scrub away the reek of coal ash.) We remember what it was like to be a small child staring up at the darkened sky, terrified, when the power plant "blows its stack"—the earsplitting roar, the black ash cloud that snows onto the modest cars and little hillside houses. We remember sledding down mounds of fly ash.

Some of my friends still live there; more of us joined the "Pittsburgh diaspora" and scattered to bigger cities and faraway states in search of jobs, education, the world. We cheer the Steelers from Philadelphia, New York, San Francisco, London, Delhi.

When we come home—for Christmas, for visits, to hug the living or to bury the dead—the Turnpike bends. When we cross the bridge the view opens up. Hills rise on either side of the

Allegheny River and two smokestacks loom high between them. When we see them, we know we are home.

There are two now. The second stack was built after I left. Unlike the old stack, it never seems to take a break; the tall column of dark grey smoke billows unceasingly. You can see it from anywhere in the Valley. Should you get lost on the back roads on your way to the new mall, it is there behind the hilly horizon to guide you.

As a child I tried not to look at the smokestack much, though it dominates the landscape. When you live in the shadow of something that huge and that ugly, you have no choice but to ignore it, to focus on the beautiful things, the flowering trees and carefully tended gardens at eye level. The plant has always been something of a blank space in my mental map of the town; it never had anything to do with me.

In the sixth grade I slept over at my friend Marla's house. She lived directly across the street from the plant in a second-floor apartment that overlooked its grounds. The view from her bedroom window was brightly lit, a confusing vista of chutes and pipes and machinery and coal. I had never seen inside the plant before; I was fascinated. Marla closed the curtain and said, with uncharacteristic vehemence, "I *hate* that place."[1]

There was plenty for children to explore in the footprint of the plant—we particularly liked the abandoned graveyard in an overgrown field just outside its gates, its crumbling tombstones honoring victims of the great Harwick Mine Disaster of 1905. Across the street, shiny black mountains of coal were heaped high. Up the hill in Cheswick, closer to my house, was the Bony Dumps, a vast expanse of slag heaps and fly ash, foothills to the coal mountains half a mile away. We walked our dogs there, poked around with sticks, dug for fossils. Boys darted up and down the little rises on dirt bikes, perforating the edges of the neighboring playground and soccer field with their tire tracks. Today there are condos there, nice ones, with neat green lawns growing on a thin layer of soil that covers the industrial waste. My grandfather used to say that the field was a deep filled-in pit, that if it ever caught fire, it would go on burning for thirty years. I don't know if that's true. Solid information is hard to find.[2]

My first boyfriend, Ethan, lived down near the plant, in the flat part of Cheswick by the river. Duquesne Light built us a park and named it after the pathbreaking biologist Rachel Carson, whose 1964 exposé *Silent Spring* caused a political firestorm that sparked the modern

---

1 Marla's mother Marti is featured in a film and article by the environmental group Earthjustice about the Cheswick plant: see http://earthjustice.org/features/in-the-shadow-of-a-smokestack.

environmental movement and led to the United States' ban on the pesticide DDT. She grew up on Marion Avenue near the high school. She died young, of cancer. Ethan and I loved to walk through her park with its trees and gazebos, carefully stepping around the duck shit to stand by the river and hold hands at sunset, gaudy green and yellow bubbles washing up at our feet.

***

GenOn's generosity to Springdale residents and the surrounding community can be seen throughout our small town. GenOn has donated a significant amount of money to Bouquet Park...and also to Springdale's emergency management services...Additionally, GenOn has built a baseball field, a little league field, and a batting cage for the Springdale community. GenOn continually provides for the annual July 4th Fireman's Jubilee festivities, administers general upkeep and maintenance to Agan Park, renders charitable donations to St. Mark's Lutheran Church, and makes many other monetary contributions to the welfare of Springdale Borough.

—SpringdaleBorough.com

The Allegheny Valley makes electricity, and we're proud of it. The school district for many decades shared its mascot, Reddy Kilowatt—you know, the little man made out of lightning bolts —with the electricity industry. (Reddy was retired due to copyright concerns.) Our football team is called the Dynamos.

Power is to us what cars once were to Detroit. Without it, perhaps we too would fade away, dissipating to let the trees grow wild through the rotting roofs of our little company-built brick houses on the hillside. Of course, we make lots of other things, too: paint, metal products, chemicals. GenOn isn't even the only power plant in town, but its twin stacks loom large.

---

2 For example, the EPA website returns broken links for several values of air pollution. Scorecard.org breaks down pollution data by county; Allegheny County is listed as in the country's top ten percent of polluted counties for toxic chemical releases and waste generation in all of the categories listed: total environmental releases, cancer risk score (air and water releases), noncancer risk score (air and water releases), air releases of recognized carcinogens, air releases of recognized developmental toxicants, and air releases of recognized reproductive toxicants. Often such data is not up to date; the most recent data listed on Scorecard.org is for 2002. The Cheswick power plant is listed as the number one toxic chemical releaser in Allegheny County, with 3,010,500 pounds of toxic chemicals released (a nearby steel plant comes in a distant second with one million).
See http://scorecard.goodguide.com/env-releases/facility-trend-detail.tcl?tri_id=15024CHSWCPITTS&category=total_env for a breakdown by chemical.

Why, you might wonder, do we stay? We were born here, for the most part, though some people move to town for the schools and the low cost of living. (Sooty houses come cheap.) Our parents were born here too. It was our grandparents and their parents who moved here—mostly as imported labor—from Poland, Slovakia, Italy, Scotland, and Russia, traveling on crowded ships to chase the promise of good jobs in the land of plenty (or maybe just to escape starvation). What they found, as James Parton memorably put it, was "hell with the lid taken off."

(Fair warning: Should you find yourself in conversation with one of my fellow diasporic Pittsburghers, think twice before dredging up that quote.)

Before she died of lung cancer, my grandmother used to tell me about the old Pittsburgh: how women were forever bleaching their curtains, how soot flew so thick in the air in some places that you'd have to turn on your headlights at noon, how two houses at the end of their old street once sank down through the ground into an abandoned mine, all the way to the second-floor windows. Pittsburgh and most of the little valley towns along its rivers aren't like that anymore. The city itself is being reborn, much of it green and shining, full of good food, innovative art, and funky, spacious, reasonably priced houses with stained-glass windows. We now lead the world in organ transplant science and the biotech industry. Most visitors are surprised to find it such a pretty, friendly, and pleasantly funky place.

The towns, though—well, it depends. In the towns where the mills have shut down, the air is crisp and clean. It is only old soot that clings to the aluminum siding of the unsellable houses and the spacious old churches where a few dozen little old ladies still worship. Our town is one of the lucky ones. We still have the power plants, as well as some other heavy industry. Our soot is productive soot, the hard work of our community powering the lights and televisions and iPads of the region, producing 15 percent of the electricity in the Pennsylvania/Maryland/New Jersey region.[3] Our soot is a sign of life.

***

Cheswick's mortality numbers are 87 percent over the national level (167 deaths compared with 89 expected), with the Allegheny River Valley showing high death rates for diseases linked to pollution.

—Pittsburgh Post-Gazette[4]

3 Group Against Smog and Pollution, "GASP and Reliant Energy," n.d., available at http://gasp-pgh.org/gasp-in-action/gasp-and-reliant-energy/.

4 David Templeton and Don Hopey, "'One of the Worst' Areas," Pittsburgh Post-Gazette, March 29, 2012.

A lawsuit filed by two Springdale residents against GenOn Power Midwest alleg[es] that its Cheswick plant is a "nuisance" to property owners...at least 1,500 households near the plant are beset by "fly ash, barium compounds, copper compounds, dioxin and dioxin-like compounds, hydrochloric acid...hydrogen fluoride, lead compounds" and other substances emitted by the plant.

—Pittsburgh Post-Gazette, July 6, 2012

Periodically you may hear derogatory accusations directed towards GenOn. We issue this announcement in hopes to appeal to your better judgment as you weigh these accusations against the benefit of GenOn to the community. Please keep the afore-mentioned contributions GenOn has made in mind and realize that they bring a sig-nificant amount of revenue into this community; the same revenue that goes into the paychecks of many residents and helps to sustain Springdale Borough's infrastructure.

—SpringdaleBorough.com

My mother's asthma is getting worse.

It's fueled by her allergies, which are numerous and severe—like mine. She also suffers from chronic sinus infections. Our grocery stores have all closed down, but the few remaining pharma-cies appear to do steady business in inhalers and nasal spray.

Mom's doctor orders a chest X-ray. "Good," I tell her; her latest respiratory infection has lasted so long that I'm worried she might have pneumonia.

"It's not pneumonia," she replies, "and that's not what worries me."

I know what worries her.

In 2009 my grandparents both died of lung cancer. Grammy was diagnosed well before Grand-pa; she participated in a pharmaceutical drug study and was one of a lucky few to whom the experimental drug gave a few extra years. My mother moved in with them for the final nightmar-ish year. Grammy's always-tiny frame dwindled to sixty pounds as the cancer took over. Her mind left us and went back to the North Carolina farm where she grew up; she was lucid for only a few minutes every day, and when she was lucid she was terrified. Grandpa, too, was declining; when Grammy died that August, he told us he'd be joining her soon. He was gone by October, slipping away while his children raced toward him on the Pennsylvania Turnpike.

That's what my mother fears.

We fear cancer because we can't trace it. It's not a simple equation of cause and effect. Cancer can be visited upon our bodies through an accident of genetics, a dangerous exposure to chemicals or radiation, or a slow buildup of environmental toxins—but most of the time, we don't know and never will. When it strikes us, we are filled with fear, but we are also busy. There are doctor's appointments to drive to, tests to schedule. There are expensive prescriptions to pay and health insurance companies to fight with and bosses to mollify. We have to tell our parents, our children, our friends that our lives are, at best, very different now. We are learning new terms: Carcinogenesis. Metastasis. We are forced to live in the here and now; there is little time to ask questions like *what did this to me?* and *why?*

Cancer experts, too, have their hands tied to some extent. It's difficult to study air pollution because there is so much of it; sorting out individual sources and isolating their effects is difficult. Lung cancer patients, in particular, tend to die so quickly that there's not much time to study them.[5] And there is a great deal more funding available for research into genetic and lifestyle-based potential causes of cancer than environmental ones.[6] That's why you hear the term "suspected carcinogen" so often—the pool is so vast and the investigation so new. We have many suspects but few convicted killers.

There's also a dearth of information because of the recent deregulation of Pennsylvania's electrical industry. Pennsylvania sits on top of the Marcellus Shale, a geological formation that is rich in natural gas. Gas wells clutter the countryside. The state hasn't seen an energy boom like this since Edwin Drake struck oil in Titusville in 1859. It's even more common in the remoter parts of the state (the rural region Pittsburghers and Philadelphians deride as "Pennsyltucky"), but it's everywhere.[7] The city of Pittsburgh had to explicitly ban natural gas drilling and hydraulic fracturing (the environmentally damaging process colorfully labeled "fracking") within city limits,[8] but as for our little towns ten mile away, well—go out to the Pittsburgh Mills Mall just off Route 28, or a mile or so out the back road through Springdale Township. As you make your way to Walmart (now the only surviving store nearby that sells enough staples to make Christmas cookies), take a look at the hillside behind the mall. When the gas wells were first drilled there,

5 See Sandra Steingraber, *Living Downstream* (New York: Vintage Books, 1998), 181–83.

6 Kathleen Struck, "Redirect Breast Cancer Funds, Committee Says," MedPage Today, February 12, 2013. Available at http://www.medpagetoday.com/HematologyOncology/BreastCancer/37334.

7 The Energy Information Administration reported 54,347 wells in Pennsylvania in 2011: see http://www.eia.gov/dnav/ng/ng_prod_wells_s1_a.htm.

8 CBS News, "Pittsburgh Bans Natural Gas Drilling," CBSNews.com, December 8, 2010, available at http://www.cbsnews.com/stories/2010/11/16/national/main7060953.shtml.

you couldn't miss the flames and roar of burning waste gas from the flare stacks; now the wells are unobtrusive, but you can still spot them easily from the parking lot.

*****

Making visible the links between cancer and environmental contamination was challenging for [Rachel] Carson...However agonizing their deaths, cancer patients do not collapse around the birdbath...although some cancer-producing substances—called carcinogens—are naturally occurring and have existed since life began, twentieth-century industrial activities have created countless such substances against which we have no naturally occurring means of protection.

—Sandra Steingraber, *Living Downstream*

The plant's new scrubber experienced severe corrosion soon after operation began and the scrubber was taken offline. The scrubber is scheduled to be operational by the end of March 2011. GASP [Group Against Smog and Pollution] has been working with GenOn and concerned community members about this issue and the severe noise that some citizens are experiencing. GASP...[asked the] EPA to reject the Title V Operating Permit of this plant until certain problems with the permit are corrected. Problems include the lack of a limit on mercury emissions, and the lack of all monitoring requirements necessary to ensure that the facility's pollution control devices are functioning effectively.

—*gasp-pgh.org*[9]

Since the boom began, and particularly since Governor Corbett took office, Pennsylvania's state government has bent over backward to welcome energy companies with generous tax incentives and loosened regulations. The Obama administration passed laws in 2012 that set the first-ever emissions limits for coal and oil-fired power plants; however, the new rules do not apply to existing plants.[10] There's no denying these laws are a victory for the environmental movement,

---

9 Group Against Smog and Pollution, "Cheswick Power Plant," n.d., http://gasp-pgh.org/projects/coal/cheswick-power-plant/.

10 Felicity Barringer, "For New Generation of Power Plants, a New Emission Rule From the E.P.A.," New York Times, March 28, 2012, available at http://www.nytimes.com/2012/03/28/science/earth/epa-sets-greenhouse-emission-limits-on-new-power-plants.html.

but we are truly starting from scratch, and there is a long path toward making sure that the laws go far enough and that they are actually enforced in every state and on every company.

In the meantime, one of the law's most glaring omissions in recent decades has been its failure to demand that not only emissions be lowered, but that they be monitored *at all*. A petition circulated by a group of local residents under the name GASP (Group Against Smog and Pollution) balked at the EPA's decision to allow the GenOn plant to stay open while repairs were completed on a "scrubber." The scrubber, a pollution-reduction device that had not been replaced since the stack was built in 1970, would reduce emissions of sulfur dioxide, the gas that forms acid rain. Allowing the plant to operate without the scrubber meant potentially large increases in emissions like sulfur dioxide and lead.[11] The permit the EPA issued did not set limits on mercury emissions, even though these are required by Allegheny County law. The EPA reports I found ranked the GenOn plant at number 13 in the country for sulfur dioxide emissions; I wanted to look at the mercury numbers, but the public records end in 2005.[12] For the last eight years the public has had little reliable access to information about the levels of mercury emissions near our homes. Fortunately, the GASP petition succeeded and Reliant Energy, then the owners of the plant, agreed to take steps to reduce particulate emissions during this period. Sulfur dioxide emissions records for this period were not available; in 2011 the GenOn plant was the seventh largest lead emitter in Allegheny County.[13]

I am not a scientist. I have never studied cancer cells or measured particulate air pollution—I majored in philosophy. I read EPA reports and medical papers to try to understand what is happening to my hometown—why everyone I know seems to have asthma if not cancer, why my mother is wheezing—but they're opaque and full of technical language. Perhaps this is one reason so many of us find ourselves relying on oral histories like my grandfather's: accessible, useful information is in short supply.

I know that the plant isn't the only source of carcinogens around. It's true that Grandpa died of lung cancer after living his whole life in Springdale. He also worked a variety of industrial jobs and smoked for fifty years. Who's to say whether it was the cigarettes, the air pollution, or a

---

11 Group Against Smog and Pollution, "Cheswick Power Plant."

12 Environmental Integrity Project, Dirty Kilowatts: America's Most Polluting Power Plants (Washington, D.C.: Environmental Integrity Project, 2006), 16. Available at http://www.dirtykilowatts.org/Dirty_Kilowatts.pdf.

13 Allegheny County Department of Health emissions search page, http://www.ahs.dep.pa.gov/eFACTS-Web/criteria_facilityemissions.aspx. Allegheny County Department of Health emissions search page, http://www.ahs.dep.pa.gov/eFACTSWeb/criteria_facilityemissions.aspx.

hundred other things? Even if it's certain that air pollution is to blame—a difficult certainty to come by—how could anyone ever prove where it came from? When everyone is responsible, no one is responsible.

All I know is that when we visited this Christmas, I couldn't escape the dark column of smoke that loomed over my head every moment—and now that I'm back in Philadelphia, I still can't escape it. Neither can my friends. We speak of it often, in worried discussions about our parents' health. That your sign of home and life and prosperity is also a sign of death—that the people you love, and indeed you yourself, have always been dependent on an industry that sees the lives of you and everyone who raised you as collateral damage—how can you ever escape that, no matter how far you scatter?

***

We allow the chemical death rain to fall as though there were no alternative, whereas in fact there are many, and our ingenuity could soon discover many more if given opportunity. Have we fallen into a mesmerized state that makes us accept as inevitable that which is inferior or detrimental, as though having lost the will or the vision to demand that which is good?

—*Rachel Carson*[14]

We are on the screened-in back porch, Mom and I, conjuring nostalgia. It's late summer. My daughter plays as we talk. This was my grandparents' hangout spot. There's a glass-topped table out here, Grammy and Grandpa's padded plastic armchairs, a few other plastic chairs for visitors, and lots of convenient spots to set a jelly-jar glass of iced tea. Flowering vines act as a natural curtain on the window that overlooks the backyard, but from the downhill side of the porch you can look out into the valley. We're high up on the hill; it's a commanding view. You can see the river winding down toward the Acme dam. You can get just a glimpse of the football field, especially if the lights are on for a Dynamos game, and it's a great spot for watching the borough's Fourth of July fireworks. In the fall the foliage on the opposite side of the valley is gorgeous. The eye is drawn, though, to the enormous smokestacks chugging clouds into an otherwise clear summer sky. I love it out here.

---

14 Rachel Carson, *Silent Spring* (Boston: Houghton Mifflin, 1962), 12.

Mom and I are snacking on cookies from the Oakmont Bakery.

I bring up a half-remembered incident from kindergarten. There had been some kind of industrial accident while we were at school. They didn't tell us what, but sirens blared—not the usual foghorns and fire whistles, but alarm sirens.

"I remember our class learned the meaning of the word evacuation that day, while we waited for the school buses to whisk us off to Acme," (the elementary school a mile away, where my mother works), I say. "I remember the kids being scared, but everybody was so sure they had the right explanation for what was happening. A couple kids said it was a toxic cloud. I'm not sure they knew what that meant, but they said it was coming to get us and the buses were trying to outrun it. I was petrified."

My mother snorts a sardonic laugh that turns into a cough, then catches her breath. "Is that really how you remember it? My god, you kids. Don't be silly. It was a minor little accident at a plant across the river. That's all. There was never any toxic cloud."

"Kids."

I shake my head and grab another thumbprint cookie, and we laugh. My little daughter joins in without understanding, and that sets us off—we laugh so hard tears come to our eyes. Above us the smokestack pumps out dioxin. Hydrochloric acid. Lead. Sulfur dioxide. Mercury.

There was never any toxic cloud.

An Excerpt from

A MEMORY THAT SUSTAINS ME

DAVID LEWITZKY

for David Sharpe, Bill Dendy, and Ed Callahan who were there,
and in memory of Jo Jo Hamilton and George Zamit

This is about Jo Jo, a Laughlin's regular. He lived next door: a little old guy in his 70s with sparse white hair, pale and distant eyes, a radiant, empty smile. He had a couple small pensions: a veterans pension from World War I and a railroad retirement pension. He made a few extra bucks cleaning up the place every night after last call. Jo Jo, always there in the background, always smiling, sitting in a corner or floating around, nursing a beer, never intrusive, never bothering anyone, constantly humming and mumbling to himself, perseverating Robert Burns, "As good as they are, as bad as they are, as good as they are, as bad as they are, as good as they are as bad as they are…a man's a man for all that…ah…Robbie Burns." Jo Jo with his high, sweet voice, his old man's voice, his old man's chant. Beyond that, Jo Jo didn't make a hell of a lot of sense; the words always seemed to come from a far-away place. I heard he was shellshocked in World War I. I heard he was an ex-fighter, maybe punchy. I do believe he was Jo Jo Hamilton, a club fighter from Buffalo, featherweight and lightweight, fought Frankie Erne at the end of his career and Tommy Paul at the start of his career, two great world champions from Buffalo. When I asked Jo Jo about these guys, he'd smile and chuckle, "Ah, Frankie Erne! Ah, Tommy Paul!" Jo Jo was our cherished and holy mascot.

From time to time my mind becomes an Ark that carries me back to those intense days and nights of my youth and my raw wanting. I recall an early blizzard in November, near four o'clock in the morning, midweek, a few of us sitting around, long past closing, huddling in the warmth, unwilling to venture out into the harsh and biting night. I was feeling privileged, I was a part of the inner circle. I was with the giants: David Sharpe, a dissipated, romantic figure, poet, friend of Kerouac's, ex-marine, Korean War vet; Bill Dendy, a short and rotund man with a Victorian manner, a journalist and scholar with a purple heart he earned in Korea; big Ed Callahan, a 6'5" roaring Irish bard, booming out metaphor and hyperbole and melody, sometimes all at once. These were my idols, men who had lived and suffered; their carriage, their posture, reflecting the fullness and triumph of their hard lives. The reality was that they were young men, late 20s, early 30s, not the weathered sages they appeared from my twenty-year-old's perspective.

George Zamit was half-heartedly trying to shoo us out so he could close up and go home, but stalling to avoid the cold. Jo Jo was spreading sawdust, sweeping up. We were sitting there, slumped in our chairs and Ed Callahan called out to Jo Jo, "Jo Jo, what's your philosophy of life?"

Jo Jo paused, thought a moment, looked up at the ceiling. "My philosophy of life. My philosophy of life. Walk fearlessly through life." He put on his coat and walked out into the storm. In his wake, the doorway glowed. We sat there, inspired and stoned.

In the Jewish tradition, it is said that there are always 36 just men: upright souls who live among us, who heal the world, who keep the world going, and by virtue of their goodness and righteousness they prevent us from destroying ourselves. These anonymous men are never recognized, they aren't saints or bards or rulers, but they are the pillars, the columns, that support the world.

I named my first-born son Jo Jo.

NOWHERE BUT HERE
SCENES FROM KENSINGTON

LIZ MOORE

photography by JEFFREY STOCKBRIDGE

In late August of 2009, I go to dinner with the photographer Jeffrey Stockbridge. I've met him once or twice before—he's a friend of a friend—and I've seen some photography of his, a series that centers on the interiors of abandoned homes. He tells me about the new project he's working on: portraits of the women who work as prostitutes in one of the neighborhoods Jeff regularly photographs. They're addicts, he says. They work for very little money and use it immediately for a fix. Sometimes they work for the fix itself. Jeff interviews them at the same time. He's started bringing a tape recorder.

He knows I'm a writer and asks if I'd like to come along sometime. It would help him to have someone else there to interview his subjects so that he can focus on making the pictures. I've recently moved to from New York to Philadelphia for a writing residency and I'm homesick and looking for new work, looking to learn my new city. I say yes. I have never heard of the neighborhood he mentions: Kensington. When I get home that night, I type it into a search engine. *Kensington, Philadelphia*: "A very fucked up area on the east side of North Philly which is known as the Badlands," according to the Web site Urban Dictionary.

The next week, Jeff picks me up in West Philadelphia and drives us there.

TANYA

$181 for food stamps, you know. It's like…once all that's gone, you know, I gotta come out here and make as much money as I can. And I don't like doing this, you know, I don't like being on the street unless I'm on Xanies. You know, because then, I'm…not that, that, that afraid. If you know what I mean. To do it. But I am afraid. You never know what can happen.

I went into detox in February. I was clean for five months. Those five months, when I was clean, I couldn't get a job at all. I went so many places, so many places, like K-Mart, Path-mark. Anything you can think of, I went to. I even went to the mall to see if I could find jobs. None of them are hiring.

Tanya, 2010

Flo, 2009

FLO

I go from here to there, I don't stay in one spot. He'll tell you. Harrogate Park. That's where I used to collect money, before I got ran out of town. Cops said to go back over where I was, because it's quiet over there, and the girls don't complain about getting beat up. I used to collect money. I sneak over there.

The first thing you notice about Kensington is the overpass that carries the Market-Frankford line from West Philadelphia to the Northeast. Set up on steel legs, a giant intractable caterpillar, the overpass is Kensington's center and its curse. Action and inaction happen here with equal fury: below, the action of cars and pedestrians and stores and people selling things to you—whatever you want, good for you, bad for you—above, in the tall weeds by the side of the tracks, an unsettling kind of inaction. Men and women falling asleep, gently. The train thunders past them and they don't wake up.

The El runs up Front Street and then veers northeast at Kensington Avenue; it is here that the women begin to appear in great numbers, scads of them, each occupying her own corner, each eyeing each other or, if they are friends, working in tandem, palling around. In winter they wear down coats but they still come out, in rain, in snow. They are what you notice second, and they notice you, too. When they are awake they notice everything.

The first woman I meet in Kensington is Sarah. She is limping down the sidewalk, her right leg dragging, her whole weight resting on the handle of a cane. Through the open window of the car, we hear her asking the men she passes for a quarter.

"I need one too," says one of them, and for a long time after she passes he looks at the back of her.

Jeff says, "Is that Sarah? Holy shit, that's Sarah."

We pass her once in the car. He tries to catch her eye, but she looks at him blankly. The pain she is in registers on her face. It makes her squint.

"I don't think she even recognized me," says Jeff. "She looks awful."

"Did she have that cane before?" I ask, and he says no.

We make a right and a right and a right, until we are back on the Avenue. And there's Sarah again, still walking up to men unsuccessfully, still dragging her leg. She's wearing jeans and a black shirt. Her hair is pulled back tightly. She is clutching a can of cola with a straw in it.

"Sarah!" says Jeff, and she turns around as quick as she can, while he pulls the car over. There is a certain amount of relief on her face. To be called out by name.

"Oh hey, Jeff," she says. She walks up to the car and leans in, her elbows on the rim of the passenger's side window. My side. This close to her face I can see her eyes, the color of her irises, which Jeff mentioned specifically when I was looking through his photographs. Their largeness and lightness.

"How are you?" asks Jeff.

"Not good. Gator knocked my teeth out," she says, and tenses her upper lip, revealing bare gum where several upper teeth should be. "He knocked my hip out too. You know how I had an artificial hip?"

Here her eyes well up from the injustice. "I been dragging my leg around all day. It feels like it weights sixty pounds."

"Hey," she says, "Could you give me two dollars so I could get to the hospital?"

When Jeff hands it to her he says, "This is my friend Liz. She's gonna be helping me with the project."

"Hey," says Sarah. She's nice, she smiles. She starts to offer her hand then changes her mind.

"You wanna give me a ride down the block?" asks Sarah. "I'm gonna see if my friend'll give me a ride to the hospital."

Sarah, 2009

SESS

I've been on my own, it'll be thirty years soon. Matter of fact I started selling my body before I even used. I've been all over the place. I never worked for a pimp, I just traveled all over. I'd wake up in Atlantic City, go to sleep in Boston, Atlanta, you know. These girls out here have never been nowhere but here. I would say 60% of these girls out here's mother was working. They got turned out by their mom or their dad.

I was picked up by a molester at the age of ten. I used to wait for him, he'd give me ten bucks. So, my sick way of thinking, all my life, I thought that I was a whore. But then when I started, I went bipolar. I was thirteen, I was letting guys do trains on me. I got real bad infections so I couldn't have kids. So then I ran into this lady, she was kind of like a mistress, and she got me into prostituting. I never worked for a pimp, but once I started the prostitution legitimately, like really being out there, I started the heroin.

I always thought, you come out here, you're a commodity, you try to make yourself look good. I got myself arrested the second day I was in Philly because from being down the shore, we'd walk around in bathing suits. I went and bought a bra and panties and had high heels and walked down the Avenue.

You know what? All these years I've been out here I mean, people love me to death, I'm real popular—but there's not anyone I could say would take time out and come to my funeral if I die.

I hold her soda for her. She gets in slowly, lowering her weight with her arms. I pull my seat forward as far as it will go.

There are two cops in cruisers across the street and I think of what this must look like, wonder briefly if they will follow us when Jeff drives away. A woman getting into a car. They must see it fifty times a day.

In the backseat Sarah whimpers. She cries. Her physical pain overwhelms her.

"You want me to show you some places today?" she asks. She has been acting as a tour guide for Jeff, pointing out spots on the Avenue and off it.

"Not today," says Jeff. "Next week, though. We're gonna be back."

"Just find me, OK?" asks Sarah.

We drop her off around the corner. Jeff gets out to help her, and she cannot lift her leg. She goes, "Owwwwwww." Jeff takes her ankle and lifts it for her, and then she stands. He hugs her, and she hugs him back.

"You guys should leave now," she says.

"The cops'll think you're trying to score on this block."

Today we see Flo almost immediately. She's wearing a yellow dress, an off-the-shoulder dress with pockets. And Adidas sandals. Jeff is driving a van today, test-driving one he might buy from his friend. Flo doesn't recognize the van when he drives past. It's a piece of shit. "This thing stinks," says Jeff, and he means it literally.

We park and an old man sitting on some steps tells us our brake lights are on.

"They're broken," says Jeff. "They stay on."

We walk toward Flo. I'm unsure if I should stay back or not. "Flo's a friend," says Jeff. "Come on."

She tells me the following things: she grew up in Montana; she's Indian; she lived out in the country when she was a kid; her mother sold her to a drug dealer when she was fifteen; she's been in Philadelphia since then. Is the dealer still around? No, he tried to decapitate her, he beat her up, he's not around anymore; she has liver cancer; it's terminal.

Some women are loud and chatty, eager for a change of pace. Flo is quiet. I ask her stupid things, like "Has the neighborhood changed a lot?" and she says, "Yeah. It's gotten louder."

I ask, "What was the best part of your week and the worst part?"

She says, "The worst part was I was in pain because of my liver. The best part was I got something to fix the pain."

She lives around here. She shares a place with some friends.

Jeff gives her some pictures to look at, contact sheets from other days in the neighborhood, and she flips through them. "She's a terrible person," she says about a few of them.

"Why?" I ask.

"She'll rob you."

When she finds herself she stops for a while. There are four pictures of her sitting on a park bench, wearing a cheetah-print leotard, jean shorts, a white band around her forehead, and sunglasses. "There I am," she says.

Jeff has his camera set up now. He takes a few pictures.

"You like my dress?" she asks Jeff.

"It's nice," he says. "What do you call that look?"

"Little girl look!" says Flo. "Innocent."

Kensington and Cambria, 2010

Michelle, 2009

MICHELLE

Every day I say I'm gonna get off it. It never happens. The only time I've stayed clean was when I was on methadone. I don't have any friends. It's better that way. People are very sheisty.

I had a good family. I try to stay away now.

I try to talk to a girl leaning against a wall. She's so high that she sinks slowly toward the ground over and over again. She's so high that the ground comes up to meet her, and she bows to it.

I know as I walk toward her that she will have nothing to say. Three men watch her from their places on a stoop, and as I get closer they watch me, too.

"Hi," I say. I'm holding Jeff's contact sheets in my hand to show her. This is an icebreaker a lot of the time; everyone likes to see pictures of themselves and the other girls on the Avenue. "Hi," I say again.

The girl looks up at me, or past me, over my shoulder. Her neck won't hold her head up.

"Hey," she says, so slowly that her voice disappears at the end.

"Are you OK?" I ask her. I can't help it. It wasn't what I meant to ask. She's not OK.

"Yeah," she says. "I'm just tired."

She falls toward me, quickly, and catches herself with her foot.

"Do you want to talk for a second?"

"No," she says. Not rudely. Kind of dreamily.

Nicole, 2009

NICOLE

I grew up in Delaware County. I do go back, my mom lives down there. I'm 24. I had five kids, and I lost four of my children to CYS[1]. Three of my kids are going up for adoption. One of them I have a chance to get back if I get myself together. I didn't start using until I lost my children. Before that I was clean. That's basically my story. I came up here and met some people, you know. I'm supposed to be staying with my mom, you know, but I come out here and end up staying for weeks. My kids are in foster care. I used to call them every day, now I call them once in a while. I still care though.

I'm staying in an abandoned place. It's pretty decent. No water and no electricity but not bad. I mean I guess it's better, for me, because I don't have to go hide on the tracks. Before I got into the abandoned place, I was going down to the tracks to get high and I ended up, me and everyone I was with, there were two guys that got off work and went down there to get high together. They were cousins. They did, um, they were contractors. They both shot up and died next to each other. They had their paychecks on them. Dead next to each other. And then, the place where I was going to get high, the bushes where I was going to get high in, there was a guy dead underneath there. But I called the ambulance —people had robbed him, took his cell phone and everything—and they ended up narcing him and bringing him back. So they saved him.

I got really high cheekbones. Everyone always tells me that. And full lips. This is their natural color, I don't wear lipstick or anything.

I know a lot of [the other girls out here]. When I first got out here…I'm a new face, and I had a lot of people that pulled over to pick me up, and the girls that are like really, really strung out, they had a problem with me getting picked up. They're all cool with me now, but they all wanted to fight me, and I was getting picked up left and right, and they were all standing there, no one was picking them up.

They thought that they could walk all over me. I just said, Fuck you, I'm out here doing the same shit you are. I just snapped the fuck out.

---

1 CYS is the acronym for Children and Youth Services, the agency that handles cases of child abuse or neglect.

Jeff often sees a whole family sitting outside in chairs on the sidewalk. He has wanted to photograph them for a very long time, and today, just as we drive by, a shaft of sun is pointed at them like a spotlight. It's getting darker earlier. Our time runs out more quickly.

Jeff parks the car and goes over to talk to them. They look, from this side of the street, like a tableau: mother and father sitting in lawn chairs, their eleven- or twelve-year-old daughter sitting on her mother's lap, a small group of young men on the sidewalk as well. One of them sits on a milk crate. Jeff goes over first and introduces himself, asks if he can take their pictures. The mother's in charge here, no question. Her name is Maria. She says he can take pictures but she wants a copy. Some of the young men sidle to the left and right when Jeff goes back across the street, thinking they're out of the frame. But when I see the picture later, one is caught in the leftmost side of the picture, watching Jeff, peering into the shot.

Maria and her family look through Jeff's contact sheets while he hurries to set up a shot. The light is almost gone. "Oh my god, look at her," says Maria. This is almost the universal reaction of every woman who flips through these sheets: a kind of horror, a kind of wondrous horror. *Oh* my *God. Look* at *her.*

Whoever it is, a hooker, a neighbor, all of them recognize each other, and all of them comment.

I talk to their daughter about school. She's shy and adoring.

"What's your favorite subject?" I ask her.

"Science and math," she says. Quietly. Like my sister.

They're moving. This is their last week in the neighborhood. They're sick of the train rumbling past them at all hours, sick of the hookers and their clients, sick of the crackheads that wander into their building and smoke. Maria says she doesn't want her daughter to have to see these things anymore.

"The only people we know out here are junkies. It's crazy out here," says Maria's husband Robert. But he also says something interesting, something that Jeff has been talking about. "This is better than HBO, Showtime, Cinemax combined," he says. "We don't need no cable. You don't have to watch TV. You just have to sit out here. You see drama, you see soap opera, you see violence and crime."

"You even see sex," interjects Maria. "Some things that I never seen before!"

They're both right. Kensington, while desperate in certain ways, is also thrilling. It's brilliant. It's alive and dead at once. It pulsates and breathes like something animated. The train overhead and the long dying light and the women themselves, standing as still as deer, alert or asleep, their eyes on every man in every car that passes them.

Donna, 2010

THE STRAITS
Robert Tell

From the Canadian peninsula across
the silver-blue fluid of the straits,
it seems a real city, with skyscrapers,
bridges, all the architectural baggage

of a vibrant, significant metropolis.
Rugged and mighty factory town
putting on cosmopolitan airs.
Fooling no one, but beloved none

the less. A commanding spectacle framing
the kinetic pleasure craft and freighters
cruising back and forth amidst
wet ghosts of warrior canoes,

rum runners, ferry boats,
refugees of many tongues,
and a river that gave its name in fractured
French to a fortified fledgling town

The Straits—the place by the river—Detroit.

Or

COLLECT
THE CON

the

IVE AND

MUNAL

TRUMBULLPLEX

AN EXCERPT FROM AN UNTITLED NOVEL

MARISSA JOHNSON-VALENZUELA

After awhile I no longer believed in the world in which I lived.

—James Alan McPherson

Sometimes if you stretch it so far it will be another thing. Did you ever cook something so long that it turns into something else?

—Fred Hampton

Detroit, 1998

The things a person does not know they know until they live them. She wasn't born here, but born of the complications that reared this city, it made sense.

Rolling downtown. Feeling one with the bicycle. Pedaling hard, then holding on and enjoying the freewheel. The weight of the bulky steel creaking beneath her. Navigating potholes and fault-like cracks in the pavement. Avoiding broken glass and random scraps of metal—aware of what a flat tire can do. Can see the stars in a city so dimly lit.

The neighborhood she exits is already asleep. As she turns onto the main thoroughfare, there are only a few old Fords, Dodges, Chryslers on the road. Some buildings have open signs that have been lying for twenty years. All that will be open at this hour are the corner stores called party stores. Their bullet-proof clear plastic counter enclosures, their dependable stock of neighborhood basics. White bread, bags of chips in 2 dollar or 25 cent sizes up front. Further away, the shelf of Cup O' Noodles for until the check comes. Faygo and forties to the far side. A small selection of outdated magazines closest to the door. She rides past these party stores—their glowing exterior lights and lurking men—with heightened senses, wary.

Now rolling into another section of the city, where sky-scraping buildings with their rows of empty windows watch her. Here it is surprising to see someone driving, odder still to see someone walking. Anyone would be as unsettled to see her as she would be to see them. But just in case, at her pace, by the time someone figures out what they want from her she will be gone. They won't have time to harass, question, beg or demand. And there can be a comfort in alone (as long as the inner tubes hold). The towering buildings are empty insulation, more markers of what used to be than what is. Slowly, she eases into the ride, abandoning fears and thoughts of escape routes for full engagement in the moment. Her hair catches in the breeze of momentum. The night provides respite from the sticky summer heat. Her muscles are awake now and eager to keep moving.

During part of her ride she can look right, south of the city, and see Canada across the water. Windsor glows bright, and even from here seems to taunt its clean and shiny, its tax base—projected into the night sky and in the reflection it casts in the gentle ripple of the Detroit River. To her left, a lot with a battered grey couch in a parking spot.

A city no one envied her for living in. A city no one vacationed to. A city so many people did not think mattered. Maybe it was one of the black mayors the suburbs still blamed, maybe it was the unions or the riots, or an increased need to self-medicate matched by increased supplies. Some preachers continued to blame a moral deficiency. Countless excuses and justifications for why the city had lost over half its population.

She'd called ahead to see what the boys were doing, and though it didn't sound like much, it still sounded better. She is tired of pretending like Val and Emma aren't fighting all the time, of hiding in her room listening to records so she doesn't accidentally eavesdrop.

And it meant she got to ride the bicycle. Her need for goals and purpose and tangible results makes it hard to ride simply for the sake of riding. And so, when she pedal brakes at their building, she keeps her hands on the handlebars a bit longer. In the small park across the street the lighting is eerie, half-cast. She looks up to check the street lamps, but they are all on. Are they only getting half power? Are the casings that dirty? Did somebody order the wrong light bulbs?

She turns away, pushes the buzzer for their floor and waits for the click of the lock release.

City as a glass of water: half abandoned or half full? The abundance of space provides room to maneuver, to look at failed foundations, at false fronts, at stripped down rusted framing. On good days, when the plumbing works, when there is enough food, when it isn't too cold and there is some semblance of safety, there is something about being free from all that excess, about having to look at your neighbor even if the only one is a block away. About your own resilience. Maybe if people reclaimed it, called themselves the winners because of being called losers. Because maybe, with what's been defined as winning, nobody should want to win.

Still, there were small, unorganized armies of men and women roaming the streets. People eaten away from the insides, from addiction and other self-distraction. Hollow eyes and cheeks, hollow bones. Hearts with no hurt left in them. Another breed of human or a raw version of everyone else? Pushing in any door that could be forced open to take anything that could be traded for more. Some people looked at her like they could eat her and she shrank in their gaze, trying to look unappetizing. However, reflecting later, she will wonder if all people generally look to each other for sustenance, to feel full. It was because of people that she was here.

***

The excuse was that he'd held the knob. John pushed her in, shut the door and held the knob tight. Ignacia struggled with it as quietly as she could while he laughed softly on the other side. She'd thought it was funny, too, until it wasn't, until she was on the other side of the door, unable to break through the cheap particle board. Soon, self-conscious of the noise, she stopped tugging and stood there, her hand still on the doorknob, and contemplated—how long will he wait? Nervous, she tried to be patient for the possibility that he'd let her back out. She listened carefully for any movement, but there was no sound. He didn't let go. He even stopped laughing. She was stuck with what she wanted.

She avoided looking at the bed and took a couple of steps toward the wall of windows, looked out at the city and wondered at it—the abundance of space, the ghost-like presence of a bustling past—again. She thought again about how she had ended up here, how it was both inexplicable and natural. She continued listening for some telling sound but did not hear John move from the door. Getting what you want should include the way you want it—what if this messed everything up? Ignacia turned away from the windows and looked across the room at Auggie. She'd never seen him sleeping.

She'd met Auggie, well everyone really, about three months before at Trumbullplex, a collective house, a mansion that, depending on the definition, arguably still was. The grand staircase remained, now with a loose railing and steps' edges obscured by papers, books, and random ribbons. The dining room still had its chandelier, though half the crystals had been lost somewhere along the way and some of the missing parts were replaced with sparkling trinkets: a mini-disco ball keychain, a pink sequined barrette, a fake pearl necklace. The common spaces in the house retained much of its gilded wallpaper, now fraying at the corners and the seams, peeling back from crown molding. There was even a library where everything but the books was in shades of painted blue. This incarnation of the house had begun in the early eighties and had since been maintained by a mostly revolving cast of literal and figurative runaways with no plans to go back.

Located on Trumbull Street, hence the name.

The first time she'd visited, the house, this city, that random first stumble in the door that she could barely explain to herself—because of a hitchhiker who talked different and told of a possibility of greater than—had coincided with a group dinner. The twelve-seat dining table was not large enough for everybody, so people spilled over into the adjoining living room or ate standing in the kitchen. A slow-motion musical chairs developed, everyone coming and going, but Ignacia stayed in her chair because it had a good view of the table and much of the kitchen. She didn't say much. She wanted to hear everything.

Most of that evening, Auggie had been perched on a chair nearby, his feet on the seat, his bent legs balancing his squatting body. He also didn't say much, but she watched him more than anyone who was talking. As he smoked filterless cigarette after filterless cigarette, he was at ease—let the smoke exit his open mouth at its own pace—while she tried to not stare and worried about how obvious she was.

Ever since, she'd continued to watch him. Maybe it was chemical. In a room, even when she was talking to someone else, all but fully engaged and listening, she would know where he was. Or maybe he was the right kind of nice. He explained things. He didn't laugh at her awe; her earnest.

A couple of months ago, John had intercepted one of her hesitant looks, and he'd raised his eyebrows to let her know he knew, and she'd cringed—caught.

Now here she was. Again watching him. Again half wishing she wasn't. *Fuck it.*

Carefully, she stepped over to his bed. Once there, she paused, thought about how people seem smaller when they are lying down. Her body troubled and tense. Her breath amplified. *What are you going to do—stand here all night?*

Finally, she forced herself to sit on the edge of his mattress, and her weight shifted him slightly in her direction. *Shit.*

It was enough. He woke, blinked, saw her, said a groggy, pleased hello.

"Hey." Arms crossed, she protested, "I am not sleeping on the couch."

Already there had been, in their mutual shyness, too many awkward nights that had ended with her sleeping on that ill-fitting piece of furniture.

He sat halfway up in bed, questioned, "So you're gonna sleep here?"

"Yeah."

He gave a soft, just roused smile as he reached for her.

She focused on touch, and tried to turn her mind off. They were there. It could be careful.

And it was; exploration, not conquest. His hands found her hands. Their fingers laced, gripped, then let go and wandered. The same and at the same time new.

＊

Soon Auggie paused to turn the record player on low because the makeshift walls were as thin as the single sheet of drywall they were. Again and again they heard Sonic Youth's Sister album. That night lasted longer than other nights and substantiated her belief that tension will slow down time if you let it, if you're paying attention. Despite the fact that the record continually had to be flipped over, she would remember it as a seamless loop, as haunting and surreal as the city they fumbled in.

Mouth on shoulder blade, on collarbone, on rib. They went slow until they couldn't.

Abandoned high-rises stood all around them. A city post-apocalypse except that, technically, there had been no apocalypse. So many were still here, all doing pretty much the same thing—making it their own. Living and breathing. Finding work and food.

She didn't need to look again, just knew that in the dimly lit scalene triangle of the downtown park below there would no doubt be people passing by, scurrying through, getting to where they, in their search for temporary pleasure, needed to be.

The boys had the whole seventh floor for five hundred a month, bills included. The space used to be the Detroit Time-Life offices, but like so many other businesses they'd gone, as if there was nothing left to report. The apartment was so large they mostly lived in a fifth of it. They'd fashioned some bedrooms, a common space and a hallway kitchen with a bathroom at the end. Left three cavernous rooms. One of which had eighteen framed floor-to-ceiling windows with only a maroon velvet sofa in the middle. Another had been made into a sort of practice space, the walls covered in gradually improving graffiti and a mismatched drum kit in the corner. The third room was bare, looking just as it was, like they hadn't figured out what to do with it yet.

When morning came, the sunlight was strong and they bathed in it. Comforted by the warmth, by each other, they resisted. They were stray cats who remained on worn sheets, on mattress, on floor, in the middle of the room, as long as they could.

***

John laughed outside the door, clearly proud of himself. He wanted to make breakfast. He wanted them to entertain him. As they climbed into their clothes, Auggie and Ignacia were shy again. She looked out the window, down at the park, at the fragile young green tops of trees, more significant in the morning light than they'd been the night before, while Auggie focused on the floor in a hands-and-knees search for his socks. When they walked out of the room, she tried but failed to avoid meeting John's playful eyes.

Ignacia went to the bathroom and took the time to review. She just didn't want anything to get weird. She needed the guys as friends. She was pretty sure this was not the beginning of a relationship. Fine. Good. She took it all in with deep breaths. Okay. Okay. Okay.

In the what-if weeks prior she'd reined in her imagination, kept it close, because she'd long feared that specifically imagining something meant it could never again be that way could never quite be real, physical, exact. The theory almost proven now by the way her body could still feel his, by the difference between pretend and possibility, by the slight bruises on her skin.

At the sink, she splashed water on her face and wished she had a toothbrush as she squeezed toothpaste on her finger and scrubbed her teeth as best as she could. Both actions helped but why didn't they put a mirror in this nothing but functional bathroom? With the edge of her shirt she scrubbed at the skin under her eyes, fearing that last night's mascara—her one effort besides wearing her favorite t shirt and black cut-off jean shorts—had made a raccoon of her. She combed at her tangled mess of hair with her fingers, a futile cause. She put her fingers to her mouth and felt how her lips were tender and swollen. Still, she hoped she didn't look too obviously of the night before. As she left the bathroom she looked down at her feet, anticipating. *Try not to smile.*

John was merciful. Instead of teasing, he rambled on about the breakfast they would make—scrambled eggs, toast, greens with lots of garlic. How, on mornings like these, he just wanted waffles but damn it, they didn't have a waffle maker. Endless pots of coffee were a given.

Crumpled dollars pooled, the three of them went quickly down the seven flights of stairs, using the jog to wake themselves. With little jumps—skipping every other step to keep up—Ignacia began to ease into the day. Of course things didn't have to be weird. No big deal.

Outside, the three of them excused themselves from morning beggars and walked to the box truck parked in the alley across the street. The boys all had the same job—they drove this truck and another one, the one Nate had right now, for some suburban guy's shipping business and, because it was easier for everyone, the guy let them take the vehicles home. This truck had a big tag on the back of it, but she couldn't make out what it said, and, fearing it was somehow obvious, she never wanted to ask. Still, as they approached the vehicle, she studied the tag again, trying to will herself into reading the letters.

Once they climbed into the cab and the doors were closed, John complained that one of the guys asking for change should've remembered him. "Man, I see that guy every day. Why he gotta keep giving me the same line? That foot wasn't broken yesterday for thirty days in a row. It's disrespectful. Shit, sometimes I see him more than once a day."

Still, he raised his hand to the man as they pulled out onto the street. A careful recognition that had become, despite John's abrasive nature, habit. Nobody wanted enemies. As important as it was to keep a tough front, it was vital to acknowledge one's limitations. Ignacia guessed that some days John passed the guy a dollar or the coins in his pocket and that the guy probably recognized John plenty, unlikely as it was that one could survive without remembering which people were what.

Auggie drove them over to Cass Corridor, where the little co-op grocery store was housed in a nondescript burnt brick building with tiny opaque glass block windows and only a simple, hand-painted wooden sign as a marker. They picked out eggs and kale, a block of cheese. A couple of doors down was the bakery, more obvious with its banner and display case window, where they spoiled themselves with a loaf of rosemary wheat bread and a large cup of black coffee to share because John didn't want to wait the ten minutes until they got back to the apartment and made more.

John and Auggie greeted, in a reverse nod raise of the chin, a couple of people in each store, but Ignacia still hadn't met many people and could only smile carefully in their direction. No one bothered with introductions, and it no longer surprised her. She'd found that most people stayed guarded in their packs, their carefully carved bits of the city. Still, city as a small town, they looked right at her in a kind silence. She wondered where they all came from and how many people it took to keep this anomaly of a bakery going. The customers seemingly came out of Detroit's woodwork, drawn in from all over the city. The power of bread.

As they drove back downtown to cook breakfast, Auggie pointed out the Hudson building, though its immense size was impossible to miss. He explained that it used to be the home of the J.L. Hudson department store, that when he was a kid it'd had the best window displays at the holidays, all tinsel and golden, that it was over two million square feet, all those windows now boarded.

"They're gonna demolish it soon. Pretty sure the permits went through."

John interrupted, "You sat on Santa's lap didn't you?" Then laughed at his joke.

Ignacia looked at the massive building and thought about how much everyone who remained was marked by all that leaving. Auggie too. So many people had left the city that it changed the tone, the options, the route of the bus and the hours it ran. She was still so new, but she was beginning to feel the effects, the cowering defense, the unspoken alliance of the people who embraced Detroit as home. Many of whom resorted to joking about the high murder rate with an awkward pride as if the city had won something. It seemed everyone was caught up in the narrative, knew the facts and figures of violence and decay and were too eager to share their memorized knowledge.

It was like the city was an unwanted ex-girlfriend, who resorted to plaintive voicemails to her country, the state, the suburbs, promising she'd be good if only they would come back. And Ignacia wanted to tell her it was going to be okay—she would be better on her own, but it's so hard to be convincing when unsure of oneself in the moment. When a city's self-worth is threatened and it's left wondering about how things could have been different.

When John parked the truck back at the apartment, no one was around, not even the man with the over-broken foot.

She'd gotten little sleep but was not tired. As she hopped out of the truck, back down onto the pavement, Ignacia thought about how sci-fi novels have hypothesized how a city might be after people stopped using it the way it was built to be used—what it could be next. She was hungry and alive in a city that was supposed to be dying, about to make food with friends in a scraped together kitchen. Today the world wanted her and she wanted it.

BALLAD FOR AUGUST 27, 2012

Karla Linn Merrifield

Despite squall in the offing, | deluge in the making,

despite bridge out for repairs | by highway crew in hooded slickers,

we follow their detour, determined, | on a dirt road to our destination:

Erie-o,   Erie-o,   my darling, Erie-o.

Town on the Ontario map | of six vowels, one consonant.

In English, after tribal water: *Erie*, | plus *eau*, the French voyageur's water,

and hence this place at the end | of County Road 11 south to

Erie-o,   Erie-o,   my darling, Erie-o.

Today as great waters in their shallow | basin froth and a low-pressure system

shivers the north coast, | the Mummery Bros trawler out

of Port Dover slips | into the breakwall channel of

Erie-o,   Erie-o,   my darling, Erie-o.

It's a ghost boat of the Great Lakes | fisheries, one last relic that moors

to take on ice, bins of hopeful ice going | into heavy gale this rough day from

Erie-o,   Erie-o,   my darling, Erie-o.

Rain does not deter the two of us | as you hold the umbrellas while I
photograph two lighthouses and a blue | range light and that sea-worthy vessel
and wind-tossed cormorants and gulls | chasing chum—oh, generous is

Erie-o,   Erie-o,   my darling, Erie-o.

Here is harbor from the August storm, | a pub-café-post office-variety store,
ad hoc museum, where a waitress, slim | and fit, bare-shouldered this chilly morning,
wears arm-length lightning-bolt tattoos | and serves us stories with toast and coffee;
we commune in hospitable warmth | with a complement of locals hailing

Erie-o,   Erie-o,   my darling, Erie-o.

Over eggs and peameal bacon slabs, they chaw | about the port's heyday of coal, remark
paved-over railroad tracks became Broadway, | and disclose in a bit of a Celtic brogue,
Don't hold your breath for any catch of the day, | *this is one heckuva bruising front, eh, here in*

Erie-o,   Erie-o,   my darling, Erie-o.

But a dot on the chart tacked to the wall, | at the western point of Rondeau Bay,
on the edge of these ice-age waters, | the hamlet hunkers down, listens, and awaits
a change in the weather for the better, | and this newest if not better translation for

Erie-o,   Erie-o,   my darling, Erie-o.

PEBBLES

VANESSA BAKER

I started thinking of him again on a weekend trip to Brooklyn, hearing his *ahl cwoal you* coming out of strangers' lips. I kept thinking about the time we visited his aunt in Brighton Beach, how she cooked plates and plates of food for us, which she had to reheat because of course he hadn't remembered to tell her when we'd be showing up. She beamed at us, watching us devour the borsch and salmon with dill, and all I could say was *ochin vkussna,* smiling twice as hard to make up for my lack of words and feeling his reassuring hand on my thigh under the lacy white tablecloth. She'd chattered away happily in Russian, telling her dead sister's only son what he later translated as, "You look so happy today. So healthy! Look at all those muscles! Listen to her. She is a good girl. Don't lose this one." Her sweet, tired face, round and scrubbed of all color.

A tapping noise woke me in the middle of the night. I sat straight up, thinking it was him throwing pebbles at my windows. But when I looked outside, no one was there.

The day after the trip to Brighton Beach, his plant died, the one I had given him to make his half-way house a little more homey. He was the one with the green thumb, oddly enough. You wouldn't guess it, but he almost seemed to be able to hear the plants talking to him. Sometimes he would pick up a leaf and say, "Just look at this. Drooping. It's calling out to you, 'Save me!' Can't you hear it?" It took a long time before I could tell a drooping leaf from a regular leaf. I tried to revive his plant with water, but all it had to say was, *Oh, no, you're not tricking me again. I'm out.* That one I heard.

I kept thinking about how sometimes a day late is too late. I thought of my cat from when I was a kid, Tiffany, her shivering outside in the winter, scarfing down any food I could get her. How one time when I'd gone to visit my father, she'd vanished, a white cat in the snow, and we never saw her again. When I asked if he'd been feeding her, he said, "I ain't feeding that mangy cat!" I thought of my father when, exhausted, I left him in the nursing home for a couple of weeks to catch up at work where I was close to getting fired for helping with all of his emergencies. When I came back to visit, I found him shivering in a diaper in the cranked air conditioning. The nurses just shrugged. He was too weak to swallow food, so I spoon-fed him applesauce, begging him to swallow it. Thankfully, he'd managed to that day.

It was my day off, and I had other stuff to do, but I knew I wouldn't be able to focus on it. It was getting dark outside, and the rain was really coming down, but an anxious, expectant feeling was building in me. I told the universe that if I had to run down to the hood in the rain as the sun was going down, there'd better be a sign and, of course, the rain stopped. Even then I considered not going, but an insistent, almost nervous ball of energy in my gut was saying to me that the time to walk out the door was right this minute and not the next minute. I splashed out to the wet vinyl street and walked fast. At the subway station, as I hurriedly swiped my card and swished through the turnstile, I hoped I didn't look like a lunatic on a quest. I quickly glanced around; no one was looking. A line of people were exiting, but their faces were studiedly blank. Even if I'd accidentally flashed a wild, Jesus-is-talking-to-me look, this was Philadelphia—odds were a more significant display of batshit crazy was taking place somewhere in the crowd right at that moment. A few people ahead of me were jogging down the blue-tiled stairwell under flickering fluorescents. I followed suit. Just as I reached the platform, the train arrived.

I took a window seat. The air conditioning made it a bit chilly, and the blue upholstered seats were prickly on my thighs. I rubbed goosebumps off my arms. A handful of people rode silently in my car: a pair of medical workers in pink scrubs, a fast food employee with his uniform in a plastic grocery store bag, a man in dirty tan coveralls and boots, a mother who had managed to momentarily subdue her two small children by hissing occasional warnings in Spanish. Everyone seemed to be resting up for the next onslaught, heads leaning on the dirty walls or windows if possible. A homeless man slept stretched across two seats, knowing better than to bother the others. He stunk up the car, but no one said anything. Somehow, the two women in scrubs were scarfing down chips.

The train rumbled through the dark tunnels, the weak orange sodium lights here and there illuminating graffiti and rats, until a station came up ahead, a bright, blue-tiled rectangle like a stage emerging from the darkness. A few strangers milled around on the stage, unaware of being observed, and the train passed, closing the curtain. I wondered if that's how our lives looked to G-d, if there were one, like stages emerging in the darkness. If whatever's out there just changed the channel to tune into different stories. Then I thought, *No way, too disjointed.*

No, when G-d wants to know how we're doing, it's like wanting to know how your liver is doing. You close your eyes and kind of listen into yourself, through the dark chambers of meat. You just reach inside and feel your liver. That's what it's like. Only we are the liver and the feeling of the liver at once and so is everyone else. And that's how I felt, reaching inside the winding blackness to feel a soft but insistent bleating of pain that I recognized as Sergei. In my own gut, I could feel that somewhere there were still whales swimming around in the creaking, rolling seas. I would feel them go if they went. We all would. Somewhere their wise, round eyes were still watching over the remaining mysteries of the deep. Yet I still silently bargained with the universe, *If I'm supposed to find him, he'll be standing near the subway station. I'm not walking around Kensington after dark.*

We were humming along over the rooftops now, copper gingerbread trim turned green with corrosion, blackened windows gaping. Each one had an identical little decorative crown, houses where the workers had lived, back when workers had been needed, back when the modern world was being built. The workers had lined up neatly in the factory all day and then again at night in their beds in neat little row houses under their identical copper crowns. Despite the darkening sky, it was still light enough to see in, to see a forgotten bed or chest of drawers. The angle of the buildings seemed impudent—too straight and proud against the churning sky, not cowering away from the train thundering mere feet away. *Stay down*, I wanted to say. *You already got your teeth knocked out.* Huge metal cauldrons once used for some mysterious and forgotten industrial purpose perched in the skyline next to forever-dormant smokestacks and cooling towers.

I got off at Somerset and jogged down the steps as the train pulled away. The damp heat of the night felt welcoming for a few seconds and then hung on me. The blue steel girders hunched over the street like some giant abstract gargoyle with a hundred limbs, metal sucking metal away, the low, unearthly hum giving way to a high-pitched keening that trailed off into the whoosh of the void that had sucked down several of my lovers, even me once, but that had been a long time ago. The whole street rattled as the train passed. Here, the buildings knew their places, hunkering in the shadows underneath the monstrous steel structure, windows trembling faintly. The people hunched against themselves—slump, jolt, slump, jolt, falling down in slow motion even as they talked, the slow dance of nodding out. No one was looking for them under here, and they moved languorously in the summer heat or zig-zagged frenetically from empty face to empty face. Like some underworld human zoo, every stripe of dysfunction was hanging out in plain view, as though the girders were hiding everyone from the world above, like even G-d wouldn't look under here. Hookers sat in a row on a concrete stoop leading to a boarded up door, bruised produce at a discount, wilted hair swept into ponytails, still-good stems thrust out into the street. Maybe twenty or thirty boy-men of indeterminate age wearing nothing but jean shorts and sneakers ran around trying to sell thin air to each other. One enterprising young man had an actual product for sale: bootleg DVDs. Another apostate hustler had a gold-plated crucifix and a set of pans—*Ooh look, and a package of cheese.* A few gaunt, toothless half-naked men squatted against the wall on the garbage-strewn sidewalk, looking too tired to try. Only the giant American flag painted on the side of a brick wall served as a reminder of where we actually were.

At the foot of the subway steps, a dirty white kid in dire need of a haircut and an older black man in a wheelchair were talking. The kid saw me and squawked, "*Worrrrks.*" Then, to be sure, three times more, "*Worrrks, worrrks, worrrrks,*" like some kind of broken chicken. I walked by, accidentally meeting his sweaty, feverish brown eyes. No malice—not even any energy for malice—just dope sick. I looked away, and the black man laughed once, humph, like who was I kidding, acting like I was too good to get a needle from him when obviously I didn't live there and had come for some kind of no good. The kid said to my back in an innocuous tone, "Excuse me, miss. I don't mean any disrespect, but do you get high?"

I was about to say, *No, I'm good,* and then cursed myself for my habitual politeness, which did nothing but encourage predators. Then, just ahead, I saw Sergei, glancing back as he was about to slip behind a girder and cross the street. His gaunt face was all cheekbones. He looked like a mosquito when he was getting high, with his big, thirsty blue eyes and thin little drip of mouth hanging deflated underneath those Mongolian cheekbones. His shaggy hair had been sun-bleached a shocking shade of blond, and the back of his neck was browned so sickeningly that the creases had turned into deep, permanent wrinkles. But he was still handsome. A smile of recognition spread over his face, automatically transforming it with his street kid's habitual charm. His blue eyes sparkled and he flashed his patented half-smile that always made me think of Casablanca and fedoras tipped to the side. Then I saw surprise register as he fully recognized me, knocking a little of the bullshit charm off his face. He still had that backpack, somehow. Probably all he had—that smile and that backpack.

"Clarissa. What are you doing here?" he asked, his eyes lit up more than he could hide.

"I just had a feeling I had to come check on you," I said, reaching out to hug him, feeling it was the natural thing to do, which surprised me considering what had happened the last time I'd seen him. We both paused for a split second as we reached out for each other, remembering.

He'd called me from a pastor's cell phone and asked me to come see him; the pastor took his phone back and told me to meet Sergei at his church on Sunday morning, promising Sergei would be there. Like a dumbass, I showed up, in a pink, flower-print sundress no less. I wasn't even the Christian—Sergei was. The church had bars on the windows and all of the lights were on. No one was taking any chances here—even messengers of G-d. But Sergei wasn't there. I started walking and soon he was walking beside me, saying he didn't know why the pastor said to meet him at church, that he'd never promised to go and could he have ten bucks, a question asked after he'd already led me halfway to the weed-choked, abandoned lot where he copped. Fun walk back to the subway alone in that pink sundress after saying no. He chased me down minutes later to apologize then sat with me for a few hours, dope sick, alternately blaming me for his getting high and calling me crazy, telling me he missed me until I told him I'd had enough and called a friend to come get me. The scrubs watching me get into the car had laughed and given my friend the thumbs up, thinking I was a hooker.

Later, my friend pointed out that the guy on the phone probably hadn't been a pastor at all, of course, but I happen to think that he was. If Sergei had been desperate enough to go to such lengths to scam me, he wouldn't have planned to wait two days until Sunday to ask me for ten freaking dollars. The pastor had also said that the way to lead Sergei back would be with love, patience, and kindness, and only someone like a pastor would say something so naïve. Love, patience, and kindness had been what made me try to turn my efficiency apartment into a halfway house when he'd started relapsing instead of sending him out into the cold to deal with consequences that would have made getting high seem less attractive.

Today I was just glad he was alive; it felt really good to hold his now-skinny body next to mine and know he was okay for a few moments. His cotton t-shirt was damp with sweat and his skin felt too hot. Something was different this time—not different as in *All better, we can be together and live happily ever after*, but different as in some of the anger that churned so close to the surface had subsided. The tension was gone from his embrace. A flood of love flowed between us, as strong as it had ever been. But he shook his head, almost imperceptibly, and pulled away first.

He looked at me a little warily, as though I were trying to beguile him and he had to keep his wits about him. I saw through the mirror of his expression that he had noticed the working out I had done all summer. A jolt of cruel pride ran through my stomach as he looked at me like something he would never get to have again but wanted bad. I thought of all the things he had said to make fun of my body: small tits, pale skin, not enough ass. And he didn't really like blondes, either, *to be honest*—as if I'd asked. I was glad I had worn a short jean skirt and decided to taunt him with it as much as possible, petty thing that I am.

"I just can't believe you're here," he said. It really wasn't the biggest coincidence in the world to find someone who was trying to be found, who survived off fetching drugs and selling needles on a particular street.

"Ok, so what is it? Why am I here? Something's wrong." He looked down, avoiding my question.

"Come on, what is it?" He usually came right out with things, so I figured he'd caught gonorrhea or something.

"Well, I tore my, um, I'm not sure what the polite word for it is, but I tore my nutsack open." Sheepish smile. "So I guess it is good that you came!" Thousand-watt smile and thumbs-up sign. "Aren't you glad you came all the way to the hood to hear about my torn nutsack?"

"Yes. Brilliant. How'd you do that?"

"Well, I was trying to get over a fence, and I was, um, kind of in a hurry, and my jeans got caught."

"Is it bad?"

"I haven't looked at it in a couple of days. When it first happened, you could see that stuff was coming out, but I mean I don't think my balls are going to fall off or they would have already."

"Oh my God, when did this happen?"

He paused and I saw him calculating, eyes darting past phantom cops and crack heads taking turns chasing him, wrestling and fixing on train tracks, nodding out and waking up without his bag, finding his bag, resuscitating overdosed bums on the bank of the creek, running from thugs no one could see, fixing in weeds and abandominiums, copping for kids from the suburbs, more cops chasing him, copping for and fixing on loop with girl/girl/girl, then caught himself and looked down, guilty.

"It's hard to say. The days all run together out here. I think maybe three?"

"Oh my God. Okay, let's go to the hospital right now."

"I'm in no rush. I can't feel anything right now. Let's talk and catch up first."

I considered trying to persuade him of the urgency of the matter, but he was not one to be persuaded. And anyway, he was probably hungry.

We went to a dingy little beer and subs place with neon promo signs on the tobacco-stained walls and cock rock blaring on the radio. The place smelled like grease and smoke. A hand-printed cardboard sign said 'Cash Only'. We ordered cheesesteaks and took a booth in the corner, as far away from the other customers as possible. Sergei went to pick up the food, leaving me alone. A large woman who looked about fifty-five but was probably closer to forty held forth on orgies for an audience of two skinny, bearded men. They were eating pizza, drinking canned beer, and smoking all at once. One guy interrupted her monologue to ask the other, who was standing against the wall, "Where you livin', bud? Outside?"

"No! I'm working. Drive a truck. I hurt my back is why I'm taking the painkillers." He wore a flannel shirt and cowboy hat. The other guy just said *Hmm* realizing he had guessed what laid one or two steps ahead on the other man's trajectory.

The lady called over to me, "You guys resemble each other." I pretended not to hear her. "I think she's a crazy one," she said in a low voice. "Probably."

A growling noise made me look out the window just in time to see three neon four-wheelers, pink, yellow and orange, weaving in between lanes of traffic, revving their engines. "Yeehaw!" yelled the trucker, waving his cowboy hat. *Welcome to the Wild West.*

Thankfully, Sergei returned with the cheesesteaks and started dumping ketchup on his. He was so hungry he didn't even think to talk until most of it was gone. The subs were greasy and delicious, and I tried not to think about where or how or by whom they had been prepared. I talked with my mouth full, telling him about the weird feeling that had pushed me to come look for him. He wasn't surprised; this wasn't even the first time in our nine-month-long association that I'd miraculously found him, and certainly not the first time in his life that such a thing had happened.

Between mouthfuls, Sergei asked me about the classes I was teaching (fun as ever), whether I'd gone to the beach yet that summer (I had), and if I'd visited my family since he'd gone with me a few months before (couldn't deal). He didn't ask me if I had a new boyfriend. (I didn't. I was taking some much-needed time to reflect on my life choices.) I thought about where his eyes had always been drifting when he had been with me, toward some tanorexic brunette in a napkin of a dress, and figured he probably had a beat-up Kenzo version or two. I considered asking just to see the look of embarrassment as he pictured them but decided things were going well enough not to start that conversation.

I asked if he had a place to stay, how he got food, how he got showers. It didn't smell like he was getting many showers. He said he was living in an apartment that a prostitute allowed him to stay in while she traveled to ports unknown. There was no electricity and a toilet that only flushed with a process that involved running into the basement and shutting a valve on and then off. He said people brought food to feed everyone. This detail sounded vague—I asked who and he said the Amish. It didn't look like he had been eating much. Only a few months back on dope and it showed plainly on his emaciated face. Even his cheeks had wasted away into thin folds of skin drawn back by his smile lines. But he didn't have the mean, feral look most of the street kids had when they were fiending. His eyes still sparkled, and he still remembered to smile.

"It's good to see a friend," he said, eyes soft, and I smiled back. Then, "There are no friends out here. Just a bunch of scumbags." He wanted me to look at him with pity, his bread and butter, but I refused. I made my face a mask and faintly nodded. I eyed his plate, noting that he had eaten every fallen mushroom.

"Let's get you to the hospital."

"I gotta get well first." He tried to look pitiful, but he wasn't even sweating much.

"You're fine."

"Yeah, but who knows how long they'll have me in there. I can't get sick in there and have to stay overnight. I'd have to leave. I done it before, even hooked up to machines. What are they gonna do?

I can't be sick in there."

"Fine. I'll wait here, I guess."

"Ok, you just wait here. I have to hustle up some money first, but it won't take long."

"I'm not waiting here all night worrying about you while you get money together. And it's dark and I don't want to be left by myself here. Let me just get you a Suboxone."

"It won't work. I still got enough dope in my system from this morning that it'll just make me sick."

"Fine, I'll get you a bag of dope, but I'm coming with you. I'm not sitting here for hours only to realize you aren't coming back and then wonder what happened, and then you'll never get to the hospital. Fuck no."

"It's probably not the best idea for you to come, but okay."

Of course it wasn't, but he couldn't hide the relief on his face as I handed him ten bucks. When we got to the street, he didn't even stop, just ran between cars as they crawled along, and I ran after him. In their headlights, he looked like any junkie, running.

He was steps ahead, and I hurried to keep up on the littered sidewalk. Dark candelabras of shoes hung from the telephone wires. The storefronts' metal accordion doors were all pulled down—some for the night, some for the century. Most of the brick row houses were dark, and a few had windows boarded up with plywood. Some had windows without a shard of glass clinging to the soggy, rotting frames, like toothless gums in a mouth stretched wide in grief. Right next to these unloved and battered faces were windows with backlit patterned sheets subbing in for curtains. Did the people who lived there hear the emptiness next door? Or worse, did they hear rats running around freely in the cavernous space? Other human beings?

I was walking on the outside of the sidewalk and he switched sides, moving me to the right by the hips, explaining as he did, "Better walk on this side. When you're walking with a hooker who wants a date, she walks on that side."

"What glamorous company you've been keeping," I said, and he didn't respond. I looked up a block ahead at a girl in a mini skirt and boots and wondered if she was a hooker. The second I looked at her, she whipped her head around, black and blonde extensions trailing, and I looked away. Everyone has that sixth sense, but here it was sharpened. Even the feral cats here didn't stop to lick their paws. They just ran everywhere they went.

"You know, those girls don't have it easy," he said at last, in a gentle voice. "I mean, the pretty ones get picked up first, and then, you know, they have to lower the price. It has to make them feel like shit about themselves. And you just don't even want to know the shit they come from." Now I was the one who didn't have anything to say.

Buildings were patched with bare plywood, painted plywood, plywood patched with plywood, scraps of tin. Paint jobs abruptly ended mid-wall, like someone had started painting and given up halfway through, saying Fuck it, what's the point, I've done enough, followed by someone reclaiming the wall with graffiti anyway. Chain-link patched with wooden fences patched with sheets of tin. Barbed wire trailed like vines over all of it. Chicken wire. Sidewalks strewn with garbage. Lurid, glowing signs advertised easy successes: green-and-yellow 'Cash for Gold', red dragons snaking over a yellow background reading 'Yum Yum Chinese Take Out', blue-and-red 'Men Hair Cuts $5'. And on an unlit black-and-white sign with a corner smashed in, the word 'Flowers' in a script too fancy these days for anything but a funeral home.

It was hard to keep up with Sergei. He led me down some side streets, and it seemed like we were kind of going back the way we came. Was he avoiding a certain block? The creek was up ahead, half-assedly blocked off by concrete highway dividers and a metal fence with holes where paths had been worn in the dirt. Litter covered the ground like leaves. This was where Sergei went to fix sometimes, and he said hookers went there to trick.

"Wait here," he said, already walking away.

"I'm not waiting here by myself."

He looked at me, annoyed, then caught himself and softened. "This is a good area. Look, that's a retirement home or something."

"We're standing on Gurney Street, for fuck's sake. No."

"Okay, come on, but you'd be better off here." He was too close to getting high to get mad.

He led me down some more side streets and we passed a guy in sweats who looked me over fiercely with sharp black eyes before telling Sergei, "Gimme cigarette," which he did, wordlessly. We were standing by a vacant lot overgrown with weeds. At the back of the lot was a tarp thrown over a back porch where some figures were moving around. Sergei said, "Wait here," already crossing the lot, not looking back. I walked away from the lookout on the corner, not feeling a friendly vibe. A lookout stood on each street, six in all, tensely waiting for someone they hoped wasn't coming. The setup looked like some bizarro baseball game. They began to look me up and down. They called something to each other in Spanish and laughed. I was glad I didn't understand Spanish. I started playing with my phone.

"Miss." *Crap.* "Miss!" The lookout on the other end of the street was calling to me, in a polite tone. This one was skinnier than the other and wearing basketball shorts and no shirt.

"You better not stand aroun' there like that or cops is gonna come."

I nodded and started walking back the way I'd come when, thankfully, Sergei came back out and we walked quickly.

"She don't know," he said to the scowling lookout in sweats. He was laughing nervously but the lookout didn't smile.

"Gimme cigarette," he said, and Sergei did. It was the last one in his pack. He led me toward the creek bridge and said to wait.

"No!" I shouted, but he was already running down the embankment and disappearing behind some brush. I could see the top of a makeshift tent made out of a tarp. I hoped no one was home, or if they were they were passed out. I looked around, but no one was coming. I decided to stand under a streetlight next to a long red brick wall, as though that were any safer. Did I look like a hooker, just standing there on a corner under a streetlight near a shantytown? Most likely.

"Hey there, beautiful," called out a tall shadow about thirty feet away. I started walking the other way. "Hello! Where you going?"

Just then, Sergei came running out of the weeds. I called him an asshole. "Why?" he asked sleepily, but with no concern. He had the look of dope, now. When he'd been sick, the light in his eyes had still given him some life. But now his face was slack and expressionless, like a baby's before it learns to smile. The dope seemed to pull him back to that place, further and further, smoothing out the lines of worry and care, smoothing out the features, taking him to a place before the features had been fully formed. His lips, now a guileless line, innocent of any tricky shapes they could form, hung faintly open. His eyes were halfway here and halfway in some other milky, cloudy, seminal place. For a second, his face was cradled in G-d's hands, and his body hung below limply.

"Forget it," I said.

"Forget what?" he asked, looking at me but past me. His milk-white face, a petal turned up to the sky. So close to nothing.

"Nothing," I said, and took his arm, leading him back to the creek bridge. Now he shuffled at my side aimlessly, and I was the one hurrying him to keep up.

"Where's the hospital?" I asked, and he paused for a second like he was remembering.

"I think we gotta go this way," he said sleepily. I didn't have a ton of faith in that. Suddenly, the realization hit me that we were walking next to something truly massive, something tall and gray like a stretch of sky that had fallen to the ground. *But it's too close to the ground to be the sky*, my mind reasoned, reeling for an insane, vertiginous split second. It had practically sneaked up beside me, windows boarded up and shushing the place like a finger pressed to lips. What had this dinosaur been, this thing that took up an entire city block and dwarfed all the others? A factory of some sort, but what kind?

"What's this building?" I asked Sergei.

He looked at the building and then at me, as if trying to figure out why I would ask such a question. "It's just an old, empty building They're all over the place." He wasn't actually fucked up any more. That euphoric moment right after he'd shot up had probably been produced more by conditioning than anything else. One shot was not going to get him loaded, the way he was. Which meant we might actually make it into the hospital.

Soon we were out on Lehigh Avenue, and when I saw the lights and cars, I sighed with relief. The hospital itself looked like a castle, a brownstone fortress of health, sanity, and hygiene. I feared he would find some reason to stall at the last second, like he had when I had taken him there for detox, but he went with me into the bright lights made brighter by a shock of air conditioning and sterile white walls. The burly security guard ran our bags through an X-ray machine and began to unzip Sergei's backpack.

"Careful, man, I don't know what's in there," Sergei said, meaning needles. The man nodded, knowing exactly what he meant, and used a ruler to poke around. He walked us through the metal detector, me first, then Sergei. I told Sergei to go check in at the counter and took a seat in the corner. Then I got up and slathered anti-microbial lotion on my hands and arms up to the elbow. I resisted the urge to do it twice.

The waiting room was filled with Kenzo's walking wounded. A dirty elderly man in tatters sat in a wheelchair telling no one, "I can't feel my foot! My foot died!" A young couple was whispering to each other frantically. The man's hand was wrapped in a blood-soaked kitchen towel. A street kid with greasy, shoulder-length light brown hair and a tattooed tear was staring right at me. When Sergei came back, the kid came over and said hi to him.

"Hey man, haven't seen you in a couple days." Then he whispered something in Sergei's ear, and Sergei laughed and shook his head. "Did you hear Chance got bricked?" The kid's face was animated by the excitement of relaying the big news. "Yeah. He's brain damaged now. All drooling and shit. It was Nickie's man. Found out about Chance and Nickie and bam."

The new thing to do in Kensington, according to Sergei and various people I'd met in the waiting room at a different detox facility, was to sneak up behind someone you didn't like and smash them in the head with a brick. Sergei looked over at me, laughing and mock-cringing in embarrassment at his associate.

"Crazy," Sergei said to the guy.

"Yo, man, look at this shit." He thrust his arm out to reveal a red, festering abscess. "They scraped it out a week or two ago, but it don't look good."

"Nope. Well, we're just catching up here," Sergei said breezily.

"Oh, right, right," the guy said. "I was just about to go have a smoke. You got a loosie?" Sergei shook his head and said he was sorry he didn't. "Miss, nice meeting you."

I could tell he was thinking about outstretching a hand for me to shake. He recoiled a bit and I realized that in my annoyance, I was looking at him with a face flat of all affect, but staring a little too hard, this kind of crazy blank face that I used to always wear when I was young. It was almost like a tic, a habit that I was liable to fall back into if I didn't catch it and remember to put on a more animated, feminine, cheerful arrangement of my features. It was a look that said *I see that you're a creep-o, and also, there's nothing here for you to play with*. But this was the kind of place I'd lived when I'd started wearing that look, and this was the kind of creep-o it was designed to deter, and it worked. The kid left. How easy, how comfortable it was to slip into my old skin. Like visiting one's hometown and picking up the old accent. The world where one expects decent and positive responses from perfect strangers seemed not just far away but improbable. Had I really gone to college and learned to smile at complete strangers for no other reason than that they were walking along the same tree-lined path as me?

Sergei said, "Show me pictures. From this summer. I know you have some on your phone. I want to be somewhere else for a few minutes." So I showed him my beach photos, the only new ones I had. Again, I felt a stab of petty pride as I could see him ruing his decision to get back on dope. It didn't matter that I had left him. It had felt to me that he'd had a mistress, even though it was just a white powder. It didn't matter that his decision to get back on dope had really been maybe one-tenth decision and nine-tenths brain chemistry. It didn't matter that he was living on the streets, hooked on dope, dirty, worn down, injured. It didn't matter that I didn't want him back, that I knew two hundred and ten percent that I couldn't handle the havoc he would wreak on my life. I wanted to know that he sorely regretted never being able to fuck me again, wanted him to regret every unkind word he had ever said about my ass. I am a petty, vain thing.

Then he looked unbearably sad, and I even saw tears well up in his eyes, a rare thing for him and unheard of on dope.

"What is it?" I asked, feeling shame for taunting him.

"It just felt like a normal moment there. I felt like a real person for a minute there. I forgot I was a junkie." That brought tears to my eyes, too, and I hugged his arm. He wasn't being melodramatic, for once. I'd had those moments, too, back when I was hooked, where for just a minute or two I'd been distracted enough to forget. Maybe watching a movie or reading a book or something. And then it always hit me, the weight of a million, billion pounds of days of waiting to get loaded, of never forgetting heroin for more than a minute or two. The sickness that felt like too much to bear for even a moment would wake me up every morning for the rest of my probably truncated life, or so I had thought. The terror of those mental shackles wasn't something I could remember exactly after the fact. The actual feeling was a panic attack.

"You could quit. I did."

"Someday maybe."

We watched the Summer Olympics on TV, and I pointed out that one of the volleyball players looked just like his sister. I instantly regretted saying it, but he smiled generously. I hugged his arm more tightly. Soon he was called in and I went with him out of a habit of watching him during important things like this transition so that he wouldn't run off. When we were in the hospital room, the nurse, a plush, smiling woman with bouncy red curls, asked rather delicately if I wanted to stay with him, which seemed to us like a hint that it might be more comfortable if I left. "She's gonna stay with me," he said, and gave me another generous smile. The nurse nodded her okay, gave him a gown to put on and left. I felt a strange, warm burst of pride at that, as though we had been officially deemed family by the medical establishment. It seemed only fair that he got to have someone, too.

He stood by the bed, holding the gown, looking down. "Will you do me a favor and not look at me? I don't want you to see me like this. I got really skinny."

I had never seen him act self-consciously before. "Yeah, of course, but don't worry about it. You're fine."

The rude smell of sweat cut through the antiseptic hospital smell. I heard him get into the bed and under the sheet, and again I smelled bleach and cotton.

"Okay, you can look now," he said. His shoulders were bony and slumped; he looked small in the middle of the bed. He must have caught me pitying him because he smiled a dimpled smile and picked at his gown, saying, "Look, a pocket in the middle of this thing. What do I put in here?" There was a pocket sewn randomly over his chest, cocked at an angle that ensured it would never hold anything in.

I walked across the room and sat next to him. I stuck my hand in the pocket, and we sat like that until the doctor came in.

TOM WAS AN EPILEPTIC

Clinton B. Ambs

Tom was an epileptic
Northbound on the 9:47 to Penn Station.
Promised to press the buttons for me
On the ticket machine
In return for a gold dollar.
Sacagawea (or maybe it was his
Brother Clint in Stamford, Connecticut)
Promised his golden heart
A brand new walkman for Christmas Day.
Said the choo-choo train man was
Already holding his ticket for him.
His motherfuckin' big ride was next week.

Tom was an epileptic.
Said he had a seizure on that very
Same bench last week.
Called the hospital and warned them
It would happen.
Then seconds later hit the ground convulsing.
Said he just got out of the hospital.
Knee still hurt from the morphine.
Thought it was made from opium.
Promised him a nice sleep in the back of the train
Where no one would bother him.

Tom was an epileptic.
Twenty years ago his friend
Gary played footsie with
Oncoming trains on a track near Newark.
One day he slipped and the 8:38
Broke his foot in nineteen places.
It hurt so bad it took two ambulances to
Take him away.

Tom was an epileptic.
Shook my hand with a pair of
Torn black mittens his sister gave him.
Said he only wore his hat because it
Was another gift from her.
Only wore it to keep
From upsetting her.

Tom was an epileptic.
Hated wearing hats.
Peeled it off his greasy grey head,
Coughed in my face when he asked
For a cigarette.
Said he was saving it for New York City.

Tom was an epileptic.
Got a one-way ticket from a
Rutgers Art Student who couldn't
Let him shiver in the train station.

Tom was an epileptic.
Said hello to every person who walked by
After and between each sentence he spoke.

Or

IMPORT
SPOR
COMPE

the

ANCE OF

T AND

TITION

MASTERING FAILURE
IN PHILADELPHIA

ADRIANNA BORGIA

I was not in the stands of Citizens Bank Park on October 29, 2008; I wasn't even in Philadel-phia. I watched the Phillies and the Rays play the last two innings of the World Series on an old, static-prone television sitting on a shelf next to my wide-window view of the Brooklyn Bridge. I still imagined that I could hear the fuck yous and boos from the fans, the guttural calls of the beer vendors, and the satisfying crunch of peanut shells underfoot. When Brad Lidge finally struck out Eric Linske, winning the game, Lidge fell to his knees on the pitcher's mound, arms raised high, either to touch heaven or to catch the wave of team members about to fall on top of him. As I watched this deluge of vindication I forgot, at least for a moment, about the Brooklyn Bridge, the dirty studio floor, the two-decade-old television, and the fact that I was miles from home.

At that time, I was not a Phillies fan in the traditional sense—or any type of sports fan to be honest. I attended games only if my tickets were free, and I watched them on television only when I needed the soothing distraction of white noise while I was working. What made that day in October so important to me wasn't pride for a sports team. Rather, Philadelphia's victory re-minded me that long, painful patience is sometimes rewarded. And for the Phillies in particular, their redemption came with the relief that nothing remains cursed forever.

It's a story the majority of Philadelphians are familiar with: Before 1987, there was a fabled "gentleman's agreement" among the board members of the Philadelphia Art Commission that no building could be higher than the statue of William Penn atop of City Hall. It was their way of showing respect to our founder, by giving him a clear view of the city. This all changed in March 1987—the month and year that I was born—with the construction of One Liberty Place, a skyscraper that loomed almost four hundred feet higher than Penn's statue. There were many who protested that the new building would set a disastrous precedent for Center City's historic skyline. However, it soon became apparent to city dwellers that other consequences were tied to this broken agreement: a mere two months after Liberty Place opened, the Flyers lost the

Stanley Cup to the Oilers by one measly game. "I'm not a superstitious guy by nature," said Sports Radio 950 talker Jody McDonald, "but spitting in the eye of one of the founders of our city is a bad move."

Over twenty years have passed since then, bringing more skyscrapers and more nerve-wracking, barely-missed championships. In 1993, the Phillies dominated their division from day one, erasing the shame of their previous last-place season. Although described as "shaggy" and "unkempt," the team won the unlikely respect of both the city and nation with their impressive line-up of formidable hitters and a precise, deadly bullpen. This promising team with "high hopes" made it to the World Series only to lose to the Blue Jays in the last inning of Game 6 when Joe Carter hit a home run, demolishing the small, one-run lead that the Phillies were banking on. I was too young to remember that game, let alone register its significance. Coloring books and caterpillars are much more interesting to a six-year-old than a heartbreaking baseball defeat.

Even when I became old enough to understand the basics of sports, the flurry of X's and O's in a playbook or the hollow crack of a ball against a piece of hickory wood never excited me. I wasn't particularly athletic, and I didn't see the point of enjoying a game vicariously through the players. I knew that I was in the minority with my indifference, especially during my last year of middle school. During the 2001 NBA finals, the 76ers were the only topic under discussion in the cafeteria, hallways, and even the classrooms. The groups of girls usually preoccupied with using fruity perfumes and finding novel ways to show off their developing breasts came into school wearing basketball jerseys over trim white tops, their bleached hair pulled up into pony tails. What I found even more interesting were the contrarians—the small group of kids who wore Lakers jerseys to school just to see how many people they could piss off to the point of violence. The spectacle didn't last long, though. Kobe Bryant, the shooting guard for the Lakers and a native of the City of Brotherly love, set the tone for the series by stating he was coming to Philly "to cut their hearts out." Although the Sixers maintained their post-season momentum in the first game of the playoffs, they were easily eliminated by the Lakers in the final four games, bumping Philadelphia up to second on ESPN's rap sheet of all-time most tortured sports cities.

I watched all of the playoff games, but none of them made any sense to me—the scoring, how penalties worked, even the overall purpose was unclear. At least basketball seemed simpler than football (it wasn't until I joined the high school marching band that I watched a football game in its entirety). I blame this partially on my father—for him, Sundays meant going to church in the morning and then eating a large Italian meal afterward, certainly not drinking beer and watching men fight each other for a goose-pimpled, egg-shaped ball. In 2005, when the Eagles finally made it to the Super Bowl, I watched it at a friend's house. All of the party-goers were wearing green—except for me, of course. Deep in a "goth" phase at the time, I wore head-to-toe black, which, over the course of the game, turned out to be an appropriate choice.

Like the Sixer's game, the Super Bowl unravelled into yet another masochistic spectacle of disappointment. After over 20 years of waiting for a Super Bowl appearance, our joy was sapped by a puking quarterback and a three-point loss—a freaking field goal. I knew the futility of hoping for a win, yet for some reason I found myself screaming at the television with everyone else. This raging version of myself would resurface once more from the primordial soup of Philadelphia failure. In 2007, while attending a Flyers playoff game against the Penguins (one of many stunted attempts at glory), I couldn't stay in my seat. I was no longer in control of myself—I had been possessed by the spirit of the fans. I shouted phrases that would have made my grandmother slap me in the mouth, participated in sophomoric chants, and found myself getting angry over something that, in the end, really didn't matter at all.

It's hard to be around Philly "phans" and not pick up their churlish, spiteful spirit. Every city boasts a "crazy" fan base—the Packers fans wear cheese hats for Christ's sake—but nothing compares to Philadelphia's extensive and controversial list of antics. Sure, most stadiums have seen hostile rioters, but how many have seen fans throw batteries at a player they despise or cheer when one is seriously injured? It's natural to scream at the other team, but in Philadelphia we can boast about not only berating our own players when they've let us down but throwing gravel-riddled snowballs at Santa. We even attack each other, one lowly man resorting to settling an argument over a call with a fellow phan by purposely puking on said phan's child. Vengeful vomit aside, there's something delightfully subversive about our reputation; we're addicted to acting out and getting away with it. Losing gives us an excuse to be outrageous curmudgeons, to relive the barbaric days when sports were expected to end with bloodshed.

In those early days, it was only in the stands that I morphed into a fan. As soon as the game was over and I was driving back home through the traffic, surrounded by the true fans still screaming about winning—or, more likely, losing—thoughts about football or hockey or baseball just fell away. The rage—rage!—that I had felt an hour before was completely gone. Whether any of us wanted to admit it or not, we already knew the outcome before these games had even started.

I realized that Philadelphia was teaching me how to fail. Losing by association isn't so bad, even if your team breaks the record for most games lost by any professional franchise (which, in 2007, the Phillies did). What is truly difficult is to be the one on the field getting your ass handed to you while a crowd of furious spectators screech that you're just a big fucking joke. I was considered one of the better players on my high school tennis team, which didn't in fact mean much as our team was known for losing. Our league culled its members from nearby, well-to-do towns populated by families who had been forcing their daughters to take tennis lessons since the age of five. I learned from these girls that a winner's view of failing is much more extreme than that of a consistent loser. I remember playing one girl who was hell bent on destroying me—her serves were agile and her hits were more precise than my clumsy backhand and my desperate returns. However, if I won even one point, she became a hysterical monster. She would hit the ball harder and aim it more cruelly. At one point, she placed the ball in a far corner, and I dove for it, knowing that I would miss it. When I picked myself up from the ground, I realized that my knee was bleeding. The cut was minor, but it had left a small stain of red on the new, very expensive court. That bloody mark was my way of reminding a pristine, snobby school that losers do exist, and that we sure as hell don't give up easily. I looked over at the girl and smiled.

When you think about it rationally, nothing is really at stake during a sports game. It hurts to see the other side walk away with a trophy while you're left with nothing but the sweat stains and shame, but this shouldn't affect the rest of your life. A fumbled football doesn't make your credit score worse, and a championship title doesn't mean that you'll have perfect kids or that a tree will never fall on your house. Thus, the outcome of any type of game only affected me temporarily—there was no lasting epiphany.

But in the fall of 2008, a strange reversal of fortunes occurred throughout the nation. In September alone, 159,000 jobs were lost and unemployment rose to 6.1%, the highest it had been in five years. The housing bubble burst under the pressure of flimsy promises, and a number of large banks and investment firms struggled or declared bankruptcy. My father worked for one of the struggling banks, and I read the papers every day to see if his company had been spared liquidation. It was my last semester at New York University; at the time, I was living near the South Street Seaport, a short walk away from Wall Street. My search for consolation in dark newsprint caused a series of paper cuts that September. I was preparing my senior thesis, finishing my last classes and applying to unaffordable grad schools. I justified this last action with the thought that the more I focused on my degree, the more I could forget about the uncertainty of what would happen after. During that same month, my boyfriend of four years, the best friend that I had in New York, broke up with me. He was preparing for med school and had little time to see me, let alone comfort me. I suspected that he had other reasons, but I didn't ask; my bitter imagination was enough to defeat me. I stayed up late every night, drinking caffeinated beverages to finish my work and trying not to cry, sleep, or dream as I waited for the sun to rise over the Brooklyn Bridge. I loved New York, but for the first time in four years I wanted to leave the avant-garde eccentricities of the Village, the electric aurora borealis of Times Square, and the borderline pretension of Brooklyn behind. I wanted to go back to Philly.

Meanwhile, as the once-thriving economy plummeted to depression levels, the two most unexpected teams made it to the World Series: the Tampa Bay Rays and the Philadelphia Phillies. For the first time, I started watching baseball games because I wanted to, not because I was being forced. I yelled, cheered, and cursed at the television despite the obvious fact that no one could hear me. After each win I was happy and hopeful, but the jaded Philly loser in my head would whisper, *Yes, they won this time, but you know that they'll choke in the end.* It was difficult for me to believe that the Phillies would miraculously break the bleak precedent set by the Flyers, the 76ers, and the Eagles. However, in the midst of my own personal breakdown, I needed the Phillies to show me that "loser" isn't a permanent label but rather one I could overcome. I didn't know it at the time, but I was following the example of F. Scott Fitzgerald, a man who knew plenty about "crack-ups:"

"The test of a first-rate intelligence is the ability to hold two opposed ideas in the mind at the same time, and still retain the ability to function. One should, for example, be able to see that things are hopeless and yet be determined to make them otherwise."

I try to imagine Fitzgerald in a baseball cap, smiling even though his team is down 10-1, and the fans in the stands are throwing peanut shells in disgust.

That night in October, twenty years of frustration, defeat, and decline instantly dissipated in a clamor of cheers. Some said it was fate; others claimed it was the culmination of our labors. But maybe it was a bit of both that finally broke the curse. Since the construction of One Liberty Place, other skyscrapers have risen above Penn's hat. Rather than a dull line of flat-topped office buildings beneath our founder's gaze, Philadelphia's skyline became dynamic and definable. In June 2007, a vacant lot in Center City was replaced with the Comcast Center, the newest building to claim aerial superiority over the skyline. During the topping off ceremony, an American flag, an evergreen tree, and a miniature 25-inch replica of Penn's statue were placed on top of the final beam. When the replica was stolen shortly thereafter, Comcast's vice president replaced it with a smaller four-inch figure.

As fans celebrated in Citizens Bank Park, one could imagine Penn listening while taking in the view from his new 973-foot post, satisfied. From my own far-off post in New York, I pretended that instead of a glowing Brooklyn Bridge, I could see a parade of fans wearing red and white pinstripes. They were celebrating with me, but also warning me, urging me to remember: *We know what winning feels like but should never forget the passion of losing.* As Jere Longman, a *New York Times* writer, said, "Here [in Philadelphia], victory is fleeting and ephemeral, not an encouraging sign that further success is ahead but a taunting hint that disaster is just around the corner in a city where defeat has become the natural order."

Even now, this cutting proclamation holds true—since our euphoric World Series win, we came close to a second, just a year later, only to see ourselves slip once more. But my most heart-breaking moment as a fan wasn't when we lost that 2009 series to the Yankees but during the 2011 playoffs. The Phillies beat the Atlanta Braves for the NL East Division title, giving them a total of 102 wins for the season and the pleasure of knocking away the Braves' hopes for the wild card. Our celebration against the Braves caused a strange reversal of fortunes during the fifth playoff game against the St. Louis Cardinals. By the bottom of the ninth inning, the Cardinals were leading by only one run. With two outs on the board, the tall, imposing Ryan Howard was our last chance. *We need one run, just one more run and we can tie.* Howard hit a ground ball, which was quickly snatched up by the Cardinal's second baseman. The collective hearts and watery, fat tears of Philadelphia fell as Howard, in a futile attempt to get to first base, tripped, limped, and finally crumpled to the ground like a wet paper doll. The image of our statuesque slugger, lying on the ground like a broken child, clutching his foot with a grimace of pain, will forever symbol-ize in my mind the complete helplessness that each fan felt that night. This is something that all fans who watched that game will carry in the dark, empty space that exists in their hopeful, complacent hearts.

But there is light, too. For every failed attempt, we can always remember the times when the Sisyphean certainty of losing was thwarted. When Lidge threw the final pitch that October, giving Philadelphia its first win since the curse, my life didn't instantly change. All my problems were still there, but as I watched the pile of players on the field, the once-losers jumping on each other, laughing, I was comforted. Failing hurts, but we know that it won't stop us from trying again. It's like at the end of *Rocky II*, when he's reaching for the ropes, about to face defeat for the second time, and he hears the words, "Get up you son-of-a-bitch, because Mickey loves you."

The only difference is that Mickey is us.

DON'T FORGET THE MOTOR CITY...

NANCY COOK

Friday: A Detroit Mood

A gray day. The smell of metal in the air. I'm feeling my age.

Henry sleeps until noon. His cell phone buzzes all morning with incoming text messages. Just before one o'clock, we go around the corner for coffee and bagels. Then we locate a *New York Times*, and Henry heads back to the hotel to catch up on e-mails and phone calls before his community economic law conference at Wayne State.

I walk around in the drizzly rain, not able to muster enough enthusiasm for much else. I might like to visit the Motown Museum or see the Depression-era W.P.A. prints on display at the Art Institute.

But not by myself. Today I don't make such good company.

***

Saturday: Channeling Diana Ross

We wake in darkness to burglar alarms. A block away, deep alto voices exchange angry curses. Suddenly, a crash: it's the sound of exploding glass. A woman's cry, in high soprano, registers surprise and fear. It's like 1967, when on a single night the Temptations, the Miracles, the Four Tops, and the Supremes all cancelled concerts. Rage was catching fire in northern cities.

Space defines opportunity: *In the still of the night, Tracks of my tears, We're dancing in the streets*. On 1950s street corners, hungry youths congregated, creating harmony. The few, the lucky, were invited into the white house with blue trim: Hitsville, U.S.A. Hot singles trickled out, made their way into the hands of slumming deejays, broke into the top forty. "Money (that's what I want), "Please Mr. Postman," "Shop Around." Diane Ross entered the house-turned-studio on West Grand a teenager with a faulty voice and latent style and walked out Diana, a diva.

Space means separation: *You can't hurry love (no, you just have to wait).* They built a concrete wall along Eight Mile Road, split the city: realtors, bankers, white politicians, all asserting the need to preserve harmonious home communities. Affirmative actions: the U.S. Supremes said they could appreciate the value of real estate, how every man wants it, how every white man expects his to appreciate.

Hitsville, U.S.A, in present time. From our third-floor window, on the unsafe side of the city, the situation is unclear. *Stop! in the name of*—. Young men are running. A cruiser drifts by, lights off, in no apparent hurry. On both sides of the crumbling Wall, properties are begging to be sold. *Baby, Baby. Where did our love go?*

***

Sunday: Ann Arbor

Less than forty miles from downtown. I-94 West to State Route 23 North, to Business 94. Two miles up, the road divides: Stadium Boulevard to the left, Washtenaw Avenue vectoring towards town. Either way, you end up in pretty much the same place.

Over fresh baguettes and brie, the history professor and the bioengineer comment on the Normandy exhibit at the university museum and compare memories of thatched roofs in the countryside, the cobbled streets in Honfleur.

With merlot in hand, our host glances out the window to the manicured lawn where brown squirrels rustle turning oak and maple leaves. "They are so fat this year," he says.
    "Means a cold, long winter," his wife, a psychologist, says.

After dessert, we two gather our coats.

    "You're going back to Detroit tonight?" our hosts ask. Emphasis on *Detroit*. Emphasis on *night*. "How would you get to Detroit from here?" one of them inquires.

CLEVELAND IS A VOCATION

ALEXANDER BARTON

Cleveland, Ohio is covered by hundred-year-old coal dust and gray skies so often launched off of Lake Erie. There are abandoned factories and potholes that could easily devour a car. Most people either know nothing about Cleveland or have only negative things to say about the city; many of these critics are, in fact, native Clevelanders. But Cleveland is where I feel the strongest pull to a place on the map. Cleveland is where I feel challenged and supported enough to find out more about why I am on this planet.

I am in a program that focuses on vocation, a confusing word that can either sound too idealistic—something only priests do—or worse, connotes nothing at all. Of course there is validity to these perspectives, but they overlook the word's beautiful essence. Its roots are in the Latin words for "a call" or "a summons." The underlying belief is that everyone, through their upbringing, passions, experiences, and education, is searching for an honest expression of how they see the world. Even more inherent to the experience of understanding vocation is that it is not a process that is done alone or that ever ends; each new experience or friend shows us new things about ourselves. Thus, we are constantly re-evaluating where we stand in regards to our fellow human beings, the earth, and our shared history.

It is a difficult and vulnerable process that engages the entirety of a person: their fears and joys, their dreams and disappointments. It is what I am trying to do with my life and it is what Cleveland is doing, too. Most of the big cities regarded as hubs of culture or finance or population or government have never had to rethink on a major scale why they are a city. When the auto industry and the American steel industries began their steady decline, the cities that relied on them as the backbone of their respective economies went with them, hand in hand.

The Rust Belt is making a comeback, and it is not because of the return of the auto or steel industries. New initiatives for more sustainable business models and environmentally friendly policies are a vital part of the new growth. Small business owners, who were once corporate management or who are just out of college, are opening new breweries, restaurants, and places to shop, making Cleveland a vibrant place to live for many. The old stalwarts, from the orchestra to the Cleveland Museum of Art, continue to support the city and make it a place where arts and culture are not just passive forms of entertainment but also job creators. The giant health industry of northeast Ohio continues to employ many as well as attract top researchers and doctors. The small neighborhood initiatives all around the city bring people together to make where they live more of a community. The city is alive with new ideas from those moving back into the city from the suburbs and elsewhere, while older communities of blue collar and immigrant families remain committed to their respective neighborhoods.

Cleveland is a city of vocation. My own sense of where I believe the world is calling me to live has been equally challenged and supported by this city. Cleveland not only brings joy to my life, but it has often held a mirror to my behavior and actions. I work for the Episcopal Diocese of Ohio to find a new purpose for the oldest church in the city, St. John's: I go out into the neighborhood and talk with people about how they think the old church and attached parish hall should be used. I was terrified that as a member of a church group I would either scare people away or get into arguments about the existence of God rather than discuss what it means to be a neighbor. But Cleveland didn't have time for my fear. The majority of people I met with wanted the space to be used to the community's greatest advantage and saw that as the church's mission, regardless of their own stance on faith.

As an organization, the Episcopal Church is experiencing a loss of population for many of the same reasons people have left cities like Cleveland. A church often reflects the nature of the neighborhood it serves. And when the stresses of keeping the church doors open engulfs the church's ability to fulfill its mission, both the neighborhood and the church are affected. Just as Cleveland suffers from having too many buildings with not enough of a population to maintain them, the church and its European-inspired stone edifices—once meant to suggest the beauty of an ethical life—now cost more to heat than to run the programming. This constant financial strain has forced the Diocese to sell many of their buildings so that the communities can do the work of the church instead of worrying about paying the bills. But it seems that both Cleveland and the church have come to see the opportunity in what first appeared to be only negative. For too long the church worried about statistical growth, just as cities focused on economic output and development investment. Both forgot about quality of life beyond the ability to fill pews or the affordability of health insurance. While having health insurance is important and full churches are good for our purposes, it is also vital to our species to have higher intentions for each generation's brief time on this planet other than longevity for longevity's sake.

The reason that new initiatives like urban agriculture have been so popular and well supported in the Rust Belt is first and foremost because they empower people. What the church and the city have at present is a prodigious opportunity to realize that their missions are inherently centered on empowering people. We are not here to control people's lives or dictate to them the steps they will take. We are here to give people opportunities to see their lives as important and capable of offering their gifts to someone else. The city, just like the church, is empowered by the people to remind us of the very thing we often forget; we live in communities in which the majority of our actions affect other people, and thus we are capable of an overwhelmingly positive impact.

The "comeback" of Cleveland is the fight to empower more and more people to see as positive what others see as negative. We know what happens to the many when a critical few decide to close up shop and move out of town. We know what happens when a critical few decide to abuse the privilege of being elected. We know when loved ones and neighbors lose their homes. Cleveland is a vocation because it takes a certain amount of courage to speak of it honestly while accepting that some native Clevelanders, and many out-of-towners, will think that you're naive for loving it. If you are called to live here, you won't stop advocating for a community that not only stands up for your right to have health insurance or a job but also recognizes your life as essential to all of ours.

Not too long ago, a woman who recently immigrated to Cleveland began volunteering with our church. After starting her own coffee company, landing a job with Cleveland's Film Festival, and working to improve a public school in her neighborhood, she came to St. John's. She donates her time because she wants our church to be a place where neighborhood youths can receive help with their homework, play games, or just be in a place where they can act their age without the harsh realities of an urban environment stopping them from doing so.

Cleveland is a vocation because it is not merely a dot on the map or one of the many cities in the Rust Belt; it is a unique energy that stares into the void of urban decline, in search of the human face with all its pain, refusing to admit that the story is finished or out of our hands.

THE **Head**

&

THE **Hand**
——PRESS——
EST. 2012

presents

$11 + 1 = z + 20$

"WRITERITHMATIC"

IF HIS FRIDGE DOOR AND FACEBOOK ACCESS ARE 20 MINUTES AWAY, HOW MANY HOURS OF PROCRASTINATION WILL JIM CONVERT TO PRODUCTIVITY IN A THREE MONTH TIME FRAME BY WRITING HIS NOVEL AT THE HEAD & THE HAND PRESS WORKSHOP?

—www.theheadandthehand.com—

CHILD R

n

EARING

I & THE VILLAGE

M. ANGELO MENA

Isaiah went with his mom to the welfare office. They'd been there for over two hours and he and his little brother were getting bored so they began throwing popcorn at each other. Isaiah chomped at the air in an attempt to eat whatever flew his way but Simon swatted his hands to deflect. More than one kernel ricocheted in the direction of a bearded gray man with a cane and a vicious-looking scar stretching across his nose. As a blocked shot bounced off the beanie that proclaimed 'Vietnam Vet,' the senior citizen scowled at the boys and began to lift his cane. His retaliation was interrupted.

"Sir? You're in the wrong line. Just fill this card out and wait over there," said the clerk to the old man. The man abruptly turned away from the kids and shifted his glare toward the speaker.

"What? I've been waiting here for four hours! You need to turn my card back on!" he said to the lady behind the counter.

"I'm sorry, sir, but you need to be in that line over there. Your card hasn't worked for a month, how did you eat?" she asked.

"I ate at the mission," he growled through his teeth. The part he left out was that he hadn't needed the card because his girlfriend had been feeding him, but then her son had moved back in with her and the guys just couldn't seem to get along. She eventually chose her boy over her man, so he grabbed his things and decided to camp out with some of the fellas under the bridge for a few nights. When he stopped at a Spanish bodega to pick up some supplies, his card wouldn't work. It took him a few days before he could get a ride to where he was now.

"We're sorry for the inconvenience," she said calmly as she handed back the card. Isaiah saw the man's neck bulge as he smacked his contorted forehead with a withered hand.

"Sorry for the inconvenience?" He couldn't handle this purgatory. He reached across the counter and yanked on the young woman's lapel. "Sorry for the…" The place immediately erupted with protest and despite his furious assault, onlookers were able to pull the man off the woman. He flailed his cane above his head as an obese security guard ushered him out of the line and toward a room in the back. "I need to eat!" were his final words before a door slammed shut. The disheveled woman wiped away some mascara and tried to regain her composure. She placed a 'Next Line Please' sign on the counter in front of her and retreated to the employee restrooms.

Isaiah slapped his little brother on the back of the head. "Why'd you go and make that guy blow up for?" he said with a smirk. Simon just bugged his eyes and sunk his head to his shoulders while rubbing the sting from the blow. Back from her teller, their mother grabbed the boys by their wrists and dragged them out of the office without a word. They made their way past the roars of the elevated train and all the way back to Huntingdon Street before Isaiah noticed that his mom was wiping tears away. He wanted to cheer her up.

"Hey mom, guess what?" She shrugged off the weight of her thoughts and turned toward her boys. "My painting is gonna be used in the mural," Isaiah continued. "Those people I was telling you about? They said it was one of the best in the whole bunch." She used a tissue to rub her eyes and she smiled at him.

"That's real nice," she said.

"Yeah, tomorrow I get to help them. I get out of class too…" His school's art teacher had applied for a grant from the city's Mural Arts Program, and they'd been learning all about Marc Chagall. Each student had made a painting based on the artist's work, knowing that a judge would choose the best as the basis of the mural for the wall in the schoolyard.

Isaiah spent the rest of the walk going on about the details of his painting while his mother simply smiled at him. Every once in a while she'd respond with, "That's great." They made their way toward Gramps's house.

As soon as she opened the door, she smelled that the cat had done something awful. She told the boys to run upstairs and wash up. Dinner that night was supposed to have been Gramps's asparagus and BBQ pork chops, but when she saw her father passed out on the couch with a bottle between his legs, she knew it was up to her to whip something up. She pulled out anything she could shove in the microwave and set the timer for five minutes then returned to the living room to begin kicking her father's feet. "What did I tell you?" she asked.

He thought it was his dead wife talking and he mumbled back, "Don't tell me what to do…" His daughter took his bottle away and he started to wake up. He opened his glazed eyes, pushed back his disheveled hair and stared. "What are you doing?" he asked as he began looking for his shoes.

"Making dinner. Don't tell me you can't smell that. Scribbles did something somewhere in here," she said. She began hunting with her nose. "Change your clothes. You stink." As Gramps crept away, she found where the cat had sprayed. Isaiah and Simon raced to the bottom of the stairs and saw that their mother had moved the sofa and was scrubbing the rug underneath. They about-faced to the kitchen table and Isaiah began divvying up chicken nuggets. Their mother wiped her brow with her forearm and pulled off yellow rubber gloves. "Don't forget, we have pudding in the fridge." Her sons were busy shoveling macaroni and cheese into their mouths.

That night, after Isaiah had been kissed and tucked into the top bunk, he heard muffled shouting.

"Don't you care about how the boys see you?"

"Ehh…they see me jus' fine," he heard Gramps say. Simon was already snoring, so Isaiah sat up, crept down the bed's ladder, and sat by their bedroom door in an attempt to hear the conversation more clearly just as the adults began to raise their voices.

"I just don't understand…"

"Thas right, you don't unnerstand, Rose! But I do…you think I don't know where you been goin' at night?"

"You're drunk. Ma always hated you like this."

"Go get whatever you need out there, the boys'll be fine…" They began to whisper and Isaiah couldn't hear what they were saying for a long while. Eventually he gave up and crawled back up into bed. As he drifted off he imagined he heard kisses and promises. He never found out what was dreamt or heard for real.

She went out after the kids were tucked away, but was back as one awoke. A man dropped her off in front of the house and Isaiah heard them through the cracked window.

"You're sure you can't?" He thought he'd heard the man's voice before.

"Shh…I told you to be quiet," she said.

"Alright, just knock on the back door and tell 'em I sent you next time," and with that, the electric window rolled up and the car drove off. Isaiah jumped out of bed and smacked his sleeping brother in the face with a pillow. He helped Simon wash up and brush his teeth before they put on their uniforms; Simon's had a meatball-sized spaghetti sauce stain. Isaiah shoved a diorama into his brother's backpack and the boys raced downstairs.

"Slow down!" cried their mother. When they reached the kitchen she was wearing her robe and had two bowls of oatmeal set on the table. They both gave her a kiss on the cheek; she smelled like coconuts and honey. She put a third bowl down for herself and sat with her babies.

"Did you finish all your homework?"

"Yeah," said Isaiah.

"Make sure Ms. Frye gets the note."

"Okay." he looked up at her and she smiled. She held her spoon and fiddled with her food as she watched the boys eat. When they were done, she took their bowls to the sink.

"I might have a new job," she said over her shoulder as she rinsed out the bowls.

"Yeah? Doing what?" Isaiah regretted asking the question as soon as he said it. She rubbed her hands on a towel before walking over to Isaiah. She ran her fingers through his hair before shaking it up. Then she happily watched him fix it right. She held onto her smile, but the boy sensed an effort.

"I don't wanna jinx it just yet. I'll tell you later," she said. Isaiah had reached an age when he understood that the surrounding world could be manipulated. He decided to let the issue go and just hope for the best. "Get goin', you're gonna be late," she said as she began shooing the boys out the door. They gave her another kiss, grabbed their bags, and waved as they ran out of the house.

On the walk to school, they passed the burnt remnants of an old factory that had gone up in flames a few weeks before. The boys remembered the days off from school because of all the smoke and how the firefighters were still spraying the smoldering bricks on their first day back. Gramps had told them that some junkie squatters probably started the blaze, but whispers on the playground blamed so and so's brother or aunt who may or may not have been high at the time. A fancy new coffee shop had opened on the next corner, and as the boys passed they noticed a guy with braids sitting barefoot on the sidewalk next to a dog. Simon reached down to pet it, but his brother held him back. It wasn't too long ago that he'd done the same thing on the same corner, but that time Isaiah had snatched his baby brother away from a 'zombie,' their code name for the addicts with sunken cheeks and sores who stumbled along in a haze. Although, the zombies didn't seem to cling to this block as much anymore, plenty could still be found under the Frankford El. The hippie looked their way.

"Hey, little man. It's cool. He won't bite." The dog trotted up to the boys with its tail wagging and began sniffing Simon's leg. Isaiah let his brother pat the dog's head before replying.

"You should keep him on a leash." He kicked away some fast food wrappers that were blowing by. Then he grabbed his brother's other hand and began tugging him away.

"You guys heading to school huh? You like your school?" the hippie asked as the boys departed.

"Yeah, it's a laugh a minute." Isaiah had learned that idiom recently and was proud of finally being able to use it in the right context. "We gotta go." He picked up his pace and pulled his brother along.

As they made their escape, more wisdom was offered down the block, "Stay in school man. School is cool!" Simon looked back but Isaiah just kept going. He didn't want to be late. On the next corner he saw some of his friends hanging out on a little playground behind the school, just off campus grounds. Their mother had told them not to play in there because there was broken glass and drug stuff around it. Herbert, one of Isaiah's classmates, was standing at the top of the slide with all the graffiti on it.

"Yo, Isaiah! Check this out!" The heels of the boy's shoes had little wheels on them; he skated down the plastic slope in a squat without controlling his speed and crash-landed on his ass. "Oww!" Some of the other kids who were hanging around laughed at Herbert as he picked himself up and began assessing his scrapes and bruises. He was about to cry.

"Looks like fun. I'll have to try it sometime," said Isaiah. His teacher would call that *sarcasm*, and Isaiah was learning to love it. "I have to drop him off at Ms. Frye's room. I'll see you inside." Isaiah left his bleeding friend behind, reached the school's entrance, and went inside. Ms. Frye was waiting at the kindergarten classroom's door.

"Hi, Isaiah. Hello, Simon," she said. "Are you going to talk to me today?"

"If you twist his arm behind his back, he'll talk," said Isaiah.

"Hopefully it won't come to that." She smiled. "Come in and have your breakfast, Simon."

"He already ate."

"Well, maybe he'll want some juice. Does he have his project?"

"It's in his bag. Here's a note from my mom." Isaiah handed her the note and waved goodbye.

"Have a good day," she said while ushering Simon and some other kids into the classroom. Isaiah went out back to the yard so he could get in his class's line. He looked at the brick wall on the far end of the playground and saw that the mural's outline was almost finished. He'd be filling in some of it with colors later, a thought that would stay with him until all the lunches were over. He said the pledge of allegiance, read a story about kids on another planet that never get to see the sun, learned a little about conquistadors, and eventually went to lunch. He sat with some of his friends.

"I hate this pizza," said Isaiah.

"You...mm...hate this pizza?" said Dang as he chewed and swallowed. "They taste like the ones from our toaster oven."

"You must buy the really cheap kind. We eat those at home all the time and this tastes way worse. Check this out," said Herbert. He pulled a thick, yellowish rectangle of cheese off the crust. It was hard and felt like oily plastic. Herbert threw it across the cafeteria and it landed on a girl's plate a few tables over. The girl immediately reported the flying cheese and within seconds a lunch aide was heading their way.

"Are you boys throwing things again?" she asked.

"No," said Herbert.

"I told you what would happen if you threw more food in my cafeteria. You three are going to the office."

"Wait, I didn't do anything!" said Isaiah

"Well, then who did?"

Isaiah knew the trap and he wanted to stay on Herbert's good side. Herbert wasn't the smartest kid in the class, but he was definitely one of the scariest. He was a sore loser too, so Isaiah generally avoided any competition or betrayal when it came to his friend. He contemplated blaming Dang just to take all the heat off, but he thought better—Dang was O.K. "We didn't do anything," he said.

"One of you did. Get up, let's go." The aide led them to the office, but only after she threatened to call Herbert's sister to pick him up right then and there. As they walked down the hall, Isaiah thought about how the flying cheese might screw up his chances to paint the mural later. He thought about faking tears if he had to be brought before the principal. He started going through his story in his head: *My art is in the mural, Mrs. P. This is the first time I was ever good at anything* (that wasn't totally true, he did fancy himself a pretty good reader), *and I don't live in the suburbs like you, Mrs. P, I live right down the block, and this neighborhood…*" He would try to cry right as he uttered the word 'neighborhood'. He'd never really tried to put it into words before, but just thinking about saying it was misting him up. He thought that he'd describe the abandoned drug motel down the block, the muggings and murders, his father…and then he'd talk about how this one thing meant everything. He couldn't miss it. He had to find a way.

The office was crowded with screaming parents. Isaiah wiped his eyes and heard a lady yelling, "Where's that little boy? I wanna talk to him!" Her arm was around a girl of middle school age who had a plastic bag of ice wrapped in a paper towel held up to her left eye. She also had a bandage taped to her forehead that was beginning to show the first signs of blood soaking through. She swooned. The lunch lady and her mother caught her and helped her to a chair. The three boys retreated through a small crowd of upset parents and made it to a magazine rack. They pulled out some National Geographics and sat on the floor with their backs against the wall. The boys watched as the mayhem in the office seemed ready to erupt. Herbert saw his older brother coming out of the Principal's office with his hands handcuffed behind his back.

"You're lucky there's cops on your arms son! You best not look at my kid again!" yelled an irate parent.

"Clinton, what happened?" asked Herbert. His brother looked up and revealed a bruised eye.

"Nothin,' I didn't do a damn thing," Clinton said.

"Nothing!?" the father yelled. "You call strapping firecrackers to a stack of books nothing? You could have started a fire, burned up everybody!"

Herbert's brother was taken away and the principal yelled at everyone in the office to calm down. She asked that all support staff escort any children back to their classrooms. The lunch lady wasn't even mad anymore, she just told the kids to get up and kicked them out of the office. Herbert put his arms around Isaiah and Dang's shoulders.

"That was close. My brother is gonna get sent away for sure. One of those discipline schools probably," said Herbert. Herbert's brother was out of control and had even smacked their mom around once. He didn't seem that upset about him maybe going away for a while.

"You know where he keeps his fireworks?" asked Dang.

"Lunch is over, I'm going outside. Remind Mr. Toledo that I'm painting today." Isaiah was relieved to be away from his friends and all the commotion. He ran out back and went over to the mural. Some of the other kids had been scheduled to paint in the morning so parts of it were already done. No one had painted his house or his upside-down floating woman, whose arm looked like a balloon string being held by a boy on a hill. Isaiah ran over to the muralists in charge, Jake and Cindy, and reported for duty. They were handing out brushes and giving instructions.

"The sections are labeled with letters and numbers. B2 stands for blue two. The cans are labeled, too." Jake pointed to a labeled polygon and then at a can of paint. "Anyone goofing off might be asked to leave. We're here to get this done." Isaiah really liked Cindy and Jake. Jake had a funny moustache and Cindy wore flowery dresses and work boots with paint all over them. He had received a big hug from Cindy and a firm handshake from Jake when his piece was chosen. They seemed to be impressed by his knowledge of famous artists like Picasso and Van Gogh. Jake said he didn't live too far from the school, but he was originally from Lancaster.

Isaiah felt pride when he laid down his first stroke. He decided to paint the house green even though it had originally been labeled R3. Cindy knew it was from his painting, so she let him express his creativity. The afternoon was spent filling in spaces with color. Isaiah was allowed to stand on the fifth rung of a ladder so he could paint the flipped around lady with a grin. When school dismissed, the mural was about three quarters done, and students, parents, and staff all marveled at the new addition to the neighborhood.

"It looks wonderful. Nice work everyone," said the principal as she patted a young painter on the head.

"We should be done pretty soon. If we work a little more after school, we should be able to finish tomorrow before dismissal. That would mostly be touch up," said Cindy.

"We were hoping that a few of the kids could volunteer to help us for a little bit longer," said Jake, glancing Isaiah's way. It was like a signal; Jake didn't want to make any of the other kids feel bad, but he needed someone he could trust to do it right. Isaiah asked if he could borrow Jake's phone to call home. Gramps picked up on the last ring.

"Hello? Who is this?" asked Gramps.

Isaiah replied loudly and clearly into the phone, "This is Isaiah. I want to stay after school to help paint the mural that I helped make." There was a long pause.

"What?"

"I'm staying after school. Can you pick up Simon?"

"You got in trouble?...you got detention?" Gramps sounded like he just woke up.

"Yes. Can you pick up Simon?"

"Jus' tell them to sit 'im next to you. You can walk him home when you're done. I got something I need to do." Isaiah's disappointment was interrupted by Gramps's second thought. "Or better yet, what time you gonna be done?" Isaiah looked at Cindy, who was eavesdropping, and shrugged his shoulders.

"Four thirty?" he said, looking in Cindy's direction. She nodded her approval.

"I'll swing by and pick you up on the way back. Four thirty." The deal was done, and after picking up Simon from kindergarten, Isaiah was back to work. Onlookers gave them compliments and the boy felt that he was doing something right. The sun began to dip behind the buildings and an orange sky lit the last of the night's labors. Simon had helped paint a tiny bit with his older brother's guidance, but by the time it was time to clean up he was too bored to stay in one place. While Isaiah was washing out his brush, Simon picked up a small roller and dipped it in a can of violet paint. He snuck up behind Isaiah and rolled a purple streak across his butt.

"Wha?! You're dead!" Isaiah chased his little brother around the cans, but Cindy grabbed him around the waist just as he snatched Simon's elbow.

"Hold on! Knock it…" he had wiggled his way free before she could finish, and the boy toppled into his little brother. Simon's body slammed into some cans and paints splattered everywhere.

"Jesus!" cried Jake as he surveyed the catastrophe. He picked up Simon. "Are you hurt?" Simon wordlessly shook his head and stared at his spaghetti sauce stain. Paint had only spittled the wall, but cans were still pouring and mixing all over the macadam. Isaiah tried to help but slipped and fell into more paint. "Thanks for your help, Isaiah, but just go home." Jake dumped a bucket of water on the spill and gave a tight wave goodbye.

"See ya later, guys," said Cindy as she grabbed a mop. The principal was not going to be happy. Isaiah grabbed a roll of paper towels and began wiping off his brother and himself.

"Stupid," said Isaiah to Simon. The four-year-old's eyes rolled as he frowned. Isaiah knew they probably wouldn't let him finish painting the next day, and his mom was going to go on and on about him ruining his and his brother's uniforms. He had to finish his painting. He held his brother's hand and they stepped back to look at the wall. "It sure is…"

"It's pretty," said Gramps. He'd snuck up behind the boys and his voice made them jump. "Which one's yours?" He smelled like cigarettes and spilt beer, but his eyes weren't too bloodshot.

"That part right there," said Isaiah, pointing.

"The balloon lady? That's beautiful. You're an arteest." He patted the boy on the back. "Maybe we should find a frame for those clothes of yours so your mama won't scream at you." Gramps held the boys' hands and as they crossed the street. "She's working tonight. How 'bout we order something?"

"Moo Goo Gai Pan!" Simon shouted as they got in Gramps's car.

"We got Chinese last time," Isaiah said as he pushed his brother farther along the back seat. He put on their seat belts, tightening Simon's so hard he winced.

As the car pulled away, Isaiah strained his neck to look back at the mural, wanting to see if it looked even better from a distance. It did.

"DARLING, WHERE DID YOU WRITE SUCH BEAUTIFUL WORDS?"

"WHY, THE HEAD & THE HAND PRESS'S WRITING WORKSHOP OF COURSE."

Or

ARTISAN
AND THE
OF CAPI

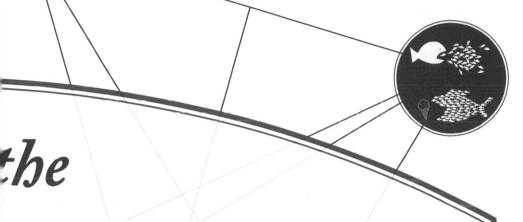

the

'S ETHIC

SPIRIT

TALISM

145

On the Conspicuous Nature OF WEIRD LITTLE BABY'S ICE CREAM AND THEIR WEIRD ICE CREAM, A Rip-Off Manifesto

JEFFREY ZIGA

EACH FLAVOR HAS its Own World, and that World is a Thing by itself for Us to find. Shouldn't We find it Together? The World of Flavors, over any border, outside any stuffy domain, any laughably impotent diagram, any entrenched smugness, outside the All of any and every class, course, or other limitedness. Dear Reader-Eaters, the Flavor World is a Public Concern of the First Importance.

It will serve The Reader to show how these Articulated Flavors come into being. Let the vowels fool around. Let the Worlds and Flavors quite simply occur, as the Sun Rises, as a Rooster Crows, as a Bell Rings…Tastes Emerge, Sinews of Sour, a Sweet Beat, some Bitter Alms, and Savory Singing. A Scoop of such Poetry is a chance to Rid ourselves of all the stale distraction, all the envy that clings to the Language of Dessert, built up there by time, erected by the Mob, put there by unseen hands, tastebuds worn

smooth by high fructose corn syrup and other falsities. We Want Flavors that Begin Where The World Ends and End Where The World Begins. Ice Cream is the Heart of the World.

We shall be Making Flavors that are meant to dispense with Conventional Language, no less than that, and then to be ultimately done with that Language. Little Baby's Ice Cream Bourbon Bourbon Vanilla. Little Baby's Ice Cream Earl Grey Siracha. Little Baby's Ice Cream Peach Granola. Little Baby's Ice Cream Balsamic Banana, Honey Miso Chive, Birch Beer Vanilla Bean, Rosemary Gingerbread, Coconut Chai, Almond Anise Amaretti, Pizza, Sour Cherry and Honey. Little Baby's Ice Cream Blueberry Ginger, Speculoos on the Loose, Sweet Potato Burnt Marshmallow, Coffee Toffee & Thai Peanut. It's a matter of Connections, of Questions, and of loosening them all up a bit, to unmake Old Connections, to find New

Connections, to connect Un-Connections. All Existing Connections are already a World and those Worlds are other people's Inventions. We do not want Worlds that other people have Invented. We want Our Own Flavor, Our Own Rhythm, and Vowels and Consonants, Consonants and Dissonance, Near and Far, Perceived Synonyms and Real & Fake Antonyms too, matching the Rhythm & Ebb & Tide and All of it Our Own. If a Cone is Seven Feet Tall, We Want Scoops for It that are Seven Flavors Complex. The Future Tastes Different.

Little Baby's Ice Cream is a Word.

It is Simple. Just a Word, and Inside the Word is a Movement. Inside that Movement: Little Baby's Ice Cream's Behavior, Little Baby's Ice Cream's Pedagogical Methods, Little Baby's Ice Cream as Aperitif and Digestif, Little Baby's Ice Cream's Literature, Little Baby's Ice Cream's Art Business, and also Yourselves! Little Baby's Ice Cream's Honoured Eaters who are reading Little Baby's Ice Cream, that Word, and its Words and Wishing that They were the Ice Cream Itself. Little Baby's Ice Cream's War on Bore Without an End, Little Baby's Ice Cream, a Revolution Without Beginning or Ending. Little Baby's Ice Cream to You, Friends, and also Poets, Esteemed Sirs and Madams and Others, Manufacturers, Consumers, Dilettantes, Experts, Evangelists, Non-Conformists, Dabblers, Clowns, Orators, Comedians, Singers, Janitors, Popes, Presidents, Big Rock Stars Who Made A Lot of Money. Little Baby's Ice Cream Pete, Little Baby's Ice Cream Martin, Little Baby's Ice Cream Jeffrey, Little Baby's Ice Cream Malcolm, Little Baby's Ice Cream's Hue, Little Baby's Ice Cream's Cry, Little Baby's Ice Cream's Color, Little Baby's Ice Cream's Ice Cream, Little Baby's Ice Cream's Little Baby.

How does one ultimately Self-Actualize? How does one attain Lasting Bliss? By Saying "Little Baby's Ice Cream." How does one become Rich & Famous? By Saying "Little Baby's Ice Cream." Eat it until you Go Crazy, until you Lose Consciousness, until you Go Bananas. How can you get rid of everything that smacks of boredom, the everyday, everything nice & right, prim & proper, unsavory, artificial, uninvigorated? Easily. By eating Little Baby's Ice Cream. Little Baby's Ice Cream is the final bars of a frenzied Soul Stomp, Little Baby's Ice Cream is the Comedy Club erupting with Feet Off The Ground and Hands In The Air. Little Baby's Ice Cream is a World Full of the Time to do Everything. Little Baby's Ice Cream in Chocolate, Vanilla, Strawberry, Blueberry, Banana, Cinnamon, Ginger, as Primary Colors in Infinite Permutations. 'Til the Cows Come Home. Little Baby's Ice Cream, Dear Reader-Eater, Little Baby's Ice Cream! And in Questions of Taste: The Tongue Is Key.

Signed,

Little Baby's Ice Cream

Food Punk // Beep Beep // Be Weird // 100% Fantasy // For Your Face Eat It Or Wear It // Singular. Vexing. Yummy. // Yummy Again! // No Rules On Planet Earth // So Good You'll Cry About It // A Moment Of Yes Flavor Blast // Encourage Brain Freeze From Birth // Welcome To The 'Get It' Zone // Posh Spazz // Be Easy // Stay Cold

CLEVELAND'S 78TH STREET STUDIOS

MAKING THE WAREHOUSE-TO-ARTIST REDEVELOPMENT WORK

or

THE EIGHTFOLD PATH TO REVITALIZATION

JUSTIN GLANVILLE

They're all over Rust Belt cities: hulking brick industrial buildings that once housed factories or warehouse space. While they'd undoubtedly become photo shoot-friendly loft apartments in cities like New York or Portland, in the softer-market Rust Belt many of these buildings sit empty, their facades eroding and roofs leaking.

The most commonly proposed solution has become almost cliché: Turn them into artist spaces! Because artists are willing to live in marginal neighborhoods and deal with faulty plumbing, walls and wiring that come nowhere close to meeting fire code and the odd collapsed ceiling, right? A coat of paint will take care of that stain, and who has easier access to paint than artists? Surely the owners of these places would welcome any kind of rent at all. Right?

Of course, the reality isn't so simple. For every building where the industry-to-art equation has met with success, an untold number of others have foundered, failing to attract a critical mass of artists or succumbing to legal squabbles with the city or state over building codes.

But considering their wealth of such structures, Rust Belt cities should keep trying. The number of artists in the U.S. has more than doubled since 1970 according to the National Endowment for the Arts, perhaps an indicator of the U.S. economy's evolution from what observers like Seth Godin call an industrial/top-down model to an entrepreneurial/bottom-up model. And Rust Belt cities may be the best-positioned in the country to capitalize on this transition. They offer the kind of cultural richness and strong sense of place that inspire creativity in more traditional artist meccas on the coasts without sacrificing space and affordability.

So how can neighborhood and business leaders ensure warehouse-to-studio conversions the greatest chances for success? An unassuming former car factory on Cleveland's near west side—now home to a thriving artistic city-within-a-city—may provide some answers.

78TH STREET STUDIOS: A THRIVING CITY IN MINIATURE

In many ways, 78th Street Studios in Cleveland is the prototypical Rust Belt hulk: a sprawling complex of connected brick buildings on a half-forgotten side street. Built between 1905 and 1922, the buildings first housed the Baker Electric Car Company (yes—electric! They ran on rechargeable lead-acid batteries). In 1959, greeting-card giant American Greetings Corporation moved its creative studios there before beating a well-worn path to the suburbs in 1989.

Dan Bush, an art collector and former display designer for American Greetings, is the owner of the complex. When he bought it in 2001 for "under a million dollars," the 170,000 square feet of space were a little more than half occupied by a hodgepodge of tenants, including a few artists and a large-ish manufacturing tenant who bailed shortly after Bush took ownership. The complex's viability seemed questionable at best.

Fast forward 12 years: 78th Street Studios is perhaps the best-known artist space in the region—home to more than 40 artists or small arts-related businesses. Bush can no longer keep up with calls from interested tenants. Every month, the complex attracts more than 1,000 people to its Third Friday events, during which tenants open their spaces (and their cash registers) to the public. Total monthly sales for the events exceed $12,000, and the events have become so popular that food trucks patrol the parking lot outside, selling tacos and pad Thai to hungry art lovers.

What happened? The answer is a combination of growing engagement and cooperation among artists to cross-promote the space, a willingness to experiment—and a few happy accidents. "I didn't have a grand vision at first," Bush says in the large office he shares with his dog Susie, a stray he rescued on a nearby street. "But the way it's worked out has been amazing."

Accidental or not, the success of Bush and his tenants may provide a blueprint for similar adaptive reuses in industrial cities. Here are eight lessons they've learned over the past decade:

1. ATTRACT AT LEAST ONE "SUPERSTAR" TENANT AS SOON AS POSSIBLE.

That may sound obvious, and easier said than done, but "superstar" doesn't necessarily mean someone who's nationally famous or has a fancy New York gallery relationship. They just have to be...energetic. (And at least somewhat financially stable—though given that we're talking about artists, some lenience can be afforded.)

The first new tenant Bush attracted was Rachel Davis Fine Arts, a young art auction and appraisal firm that had been looking for plentiful and affordable space. The firm's eponymous owner got busy referring some of her business and artistic contacts to the complex, and empty spaces began to fill with artists and galleries.

A turning point came in 2007, Bush says, when a more traditional "superstar"—the veteran Tregoning & Co. art gallery—moved in from the well-heeled suburb of Chagrin Falls. The 5,000-square-foot space provided new visibility and a center of gravity, drawing art fans from around the region to its regular show openings.

2. FLING WIDE THE DOORS!

The 78th Street Studios Third Friday events not only bring customers directly to artists, but also help build a general awareness of the building. This buzz can help attract new tenants—who, in turn, draw additional customers. Audiences cross-pollinate, with fans of one tenant discovering others. Cue snowball effect.

An important tip: As in the case of Third Fridays, name the event after the day it happens, so people won't forget when it happens. "That was the simplest, smartest thing we did," says Susie Frazier, a 78th Street artist-tenant who helps coordinate the events.

The complex also hosts an annual holiday artisan event, Bazaar Bizarre, that includes dozens of regional artists and draws some 5,000 shoppers.

3. FIND CASH TO MARKET THE BUILDING AS A WHOLE, RATHER THAN LEAVING INDIVIDUAL ARTISTS TO FEND FOR THEMSELVES.

Again, this may sound easier said than done, but marketing efforts don't need to be expensive. Third Fridays are one way of meeting this objective, and they're cheap to run (just some Three-Buck Chuck and a few snacks). But real live money can be found, too, if you're willing to poke around. Bush and Frazier applied for—and received—a $10,000 grant from the Council of Small Enterprises, a local nonprofit support network for small businesses. They used the money to implement a "branding" campaign for the property. This included a complete overhaul of the building's website, which now contains individual pages for all artist-tenants, designing and printing a visitors' map and installing street banners on Lake Avenue, the busy commercial corridor off which the studios are located. They also hired an independent contractor to manage the building's Facebook page and an email newsletter.

4. JUMP ON BOARD WITH NEIGHBORHOOD REDEVELOPMENT EFFORTS.

78th Street Studios is adjacent to Gordon Square, a Cleveland neighborhood that has seen rebirth in recent years as a performing arts and theater district. Although the complex is located some 10 blocks away from Gordon Square's epicenter—far enough away not to be easily walkable—Bush and his tenants have worked with the local community development organization to tap into this momentum. The complex is now included in marketing materials for the arts district, and opens its doors, Third Friday-style, during Gordon Square festivals and events. Trolleys help people find the building and deliver them back to the neighborhood's center.

5. DIVERSIFY YOUR PORTFOLIO.

Turns out Dad's financial advice applies to interesting old industrial buildings—not just to neglected 401K's. Building owners can protect their investment by being creative about building revenue streams and cash flow. One of the best ways to do this is by capitalizing on one of the buildings' greatest assets—their distinctive spaces. 78th Street Studios has an ancillary business, SmartSpace @ 78th, with a full-time employee who rents out several spaces in the building to weddings and corporate events. In 2012, every Saturday between April and August was booked. Couples who choose the space appreciate how the space allows their weddings to be a kind of 'Choose Your Own Adventure' for guests, who are free to wander through common areas where art is displayed. A typical wedding last summer, for example, featured a live old-time band playing in a large gallery space near the entrance. The tableau set an immediate tone of creativity and spontaneity for the festivities.

6. BE WILLING TO CARVE UP THE SPACE—AND THEN CARVE IT UP AGAIN—TO FIT TENANTS' NEEDS.

Bush spent years trying to lease a 20,000 square-foot space on the ground floor that had once been occupied by a countertop manufacturer. Finally, he faced reality: The space was simply too big for the types of small-scale tenants he was attracting. So he finally followed the market and divided the perimeter area into smaller spaces, with a larger central area preserved for events.

7. BE SMART WHEN CHOOSING A BUILDING, AND ENGAGE PEOPLE CONNECTED TO ITS HISTORY.

Romantic and cool as they may appear, some older industrial buildings may have passed their expiration date—most often due to prolonged vacancy or neglect. Because 78th Street has been continuously occupied, Bush says, it didn't need a costly initial overhaul to make it habitable. Another boon for the complex was that because it once housed the creative studios of American Greetings, it had a built-in audience of past users with a professional or sentimental attachment to the space. "The guy who named Ziggy (a comic-strip character created in the 1960s by an American Greetings executive) came in to one of our Third Friday events," Bush says. "These former employees still have a stake in what happens here, in seeing the space thrive, and they spread the word to their friends."

8. PICK A DICTATOR, NOT A COMMITTEE, TO RUN THE PLACE.

People who want to revive old brick piles tend to be idealists, and idealists like to form committees. Yet governing by consensus is the kiss of death for complicated, multi-tenant real estate projects. They need someone who lives and breathes the project and has a personal financial stake in seeing it succeed.

Bush is self-deprecating and quick to deflect praise, but tenants credit him with providing smart, consistent oversight of the space. "The whole thing is his work," says Mark Krieger, a painter whose most recent project includes portraits of children in Honduras. "It's not run by committee, it's one man's vision. And he's a collector himself, so he's got the eye." This means he not only understands artists' needs but can select who will be a good fit for available spaces. "I want to keep the standards high," Bush says—not only in terms of the art being created, but artists' willingness to participate in the community and help promote their own work and the work of colleagues.

While redevelopment strategies will vary from building to building and city to city, the ones above may point toward a brighter future for this distinctively Rust Belt architectural form—and may allow more dreams of post-industrial warehouse revival to become reality.

78TH ST. STUDIOS

Julia Kuo

A PLANTING GUIDE
for the
CULTIVATION
of
CITY SOILS,
both
DISTURBED
&
PRISTINE

Written by Nic Esposito

Illustrated by Jason Killinger

SUNFLOWERS

Helianthus annus
An annual flower that will leach heavy metals from the soil as well as present a lovely, soul-lifting display for pedestrians. Plant from seed in mid spring or from transplant in early summer. The face of the bloom will follow the sun.

RAISED BED

The perfect container for city gardening. Construct with a hard wood (cedar preferably) for the elements and fill with a nutrient-rich topsoil and compost mixture with plenty of worms.

MORNING GLORY

Ipomoea
Morning glory is considered a weed in Philadelphia, but a weed is just a plant that is tough enough to grow in the harshest conditions and the worst soil. They are tough, but they also are signs that the soil is not healthy. While making your soil healthy and removing some of these weeds, cultivate a few to climb fences and make the chain link look pleasant.

VEGETABLES

Grow a diverse crop of vegetables for each season that will bring a variety of people from your neighborhood into your garden. Give them extra vegetables and invite them for meals.

CHICKENS

Gallus gallus domesticus
A wonderful creature that will mow your lawn, control your pests, fertilize your soil and provide brown, white or blue eggs depending on the breed. Be careful of their pecking order and their propensity to escape from their coop and eat all the strawberries.

SOIL STRATA TOPSOIL

A mineral-rich soil mixture of naturally occurring elements from Philadelphia's geological past as well as lead and arsenic from the Industrial period.

SOIL STRATA DEVELOPMENT SUBSOIL

The remnant of decaying row houses and factories that were demolished and buried in the soil (standard Philadelphia practice).

SOIL STRATA PREHISTORIC BEDROCK

The layers of schist and sediment that have been forming from sand and clay for 500 million years since the super-continent Pangea broke apart.

SOIL STRATA INDUSTRIAL MATERIAL

One of the many terracotta caps that 19th century engineers built to cover the network of tributaries that flow from Philadelphia's three main rivers.

DETROIT

p. 89

p. 92   p. 126

p. 128

p. 150

p. 28   CLEVELAND

p. 60

PITTSBU

p. 5

p. 44

p. 32

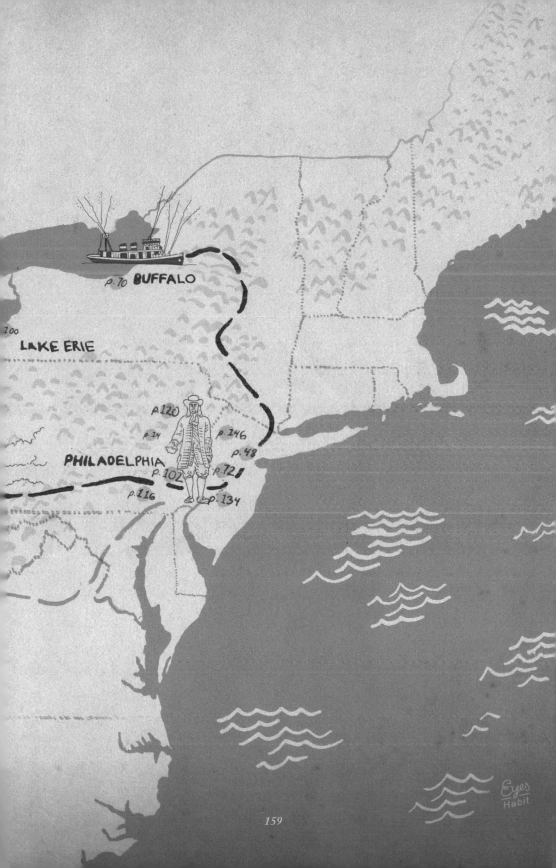

BUFFALO p. 70

LAKE ERIE 100

p. 120
p. 34   p. 146
PHILADELPHIA   p. 48
p. 102   p. 72
p. 116   p. 134

Eyes
Habit

159

the wheels of the ZODIAC

I VIRGO
II LIBRA
III SCORPIO
IV SAGITTARIUS
V CAPRICORN
VI AQUARIUS

VII PISCES
VIII AIRES
IX TAURUS
X GEMINI
XI CANCER
XII LEO

(I) 1ST HOUSE
House of the Physical
VIRGO
Belly

(II) 2ND HOUSE
House of Possession & Feelings
LIBRA
Reins (Arms)

(III) 3RD HOUSE
House of Family Ties
SCORPIO
Secrets

(IV) 4TH HOUSE
The Beginning & The Ending of Life
SAGITTARIUS
Thighs

(V) 5TH HOUSE
House of Creativity Love & Children
CAPRICORN
Knees

(VI) 6TH HOUSE
House of Work & Health
AQUARIUS
Legs

(VII) 7TH HOUSE
House of Personal Relationships
PISCES
Feet

(IIX) 8TH HOUSE
House of Crime & Sex
AIRES
Head

(IX) 9TH HOUSE
House of Futhering: Education, Travel,
Languages & Dreams
TAURUS
Neck

(X) 10TH HOUSE
House of Ambition
GEMINI
Arms

(XI) 11TH HOUSE
House of Influence: Friends, Public Affairs
CANCER
Breast

(XII) 12TH HOUSE
House of Escapism & Seclusion
LEO
Heart

Amanda Gallant

CONTRIBUTORS

Authors

Clinton Ambs Clinton Blackwell Ambs is a graduate of Rowan University and teacher of English and Theatre at Delaware Valley Regional High School in Frenchtown, New Jersey. He currently resides in Flemington, New Jersey.

John Aylesworth teaches kids in Southeast Ohio how to read, write, and survive poverty, abuse, and the difficulties of growing up in rural Appalachia. He has an M.A. in Creative Writing and a PhD. in Comparative Arts from Ohio University in Athens, where he's lived for 25 years with his wife, two boys, two dogs, and a cat named Lucy.

Vanessa Baker teaches English as a second language to adults in Philadelphia, and has also taught in China and Korea. She has freelanced for the *Centre Daily Times* and written visitor's guides to several Pennsylvania towns.

Alexander Barton was born in Baltimore to a family that instilled a deep passion for the arts and hospitality. He attended boarding high school in the Smoky Mountains of Tennessee and Transylvania University in Lexington, Kentucky. Having wanted to try and live a simpler life along with trying to be more available to my neighbor, he decided to join the Episcopal Service Corps in Cleveland, where he lives with seven other people, each of whom work at different non-profits throughout the city. He loves to talk, listen, read, and tell people to come to Cleveland.

Adrianna Borgia has lived in both New York and Boston, but Philadelphia will always be her home. Her New York friends think she's crazy for choosing the dirty, "scary" Philadelphia over the Big Apple, but they've never been inside a Wawa. Adrianna currently works in Center City, editing medical periodicals. In her spare time, when she's not dreaming of owning a goat farm or yelling at the Phillies on the TV, she enjoys blogging, reading, and making awesome Italian food.

Jackie Campbell has a Master's in English from Penn State University, where she teaches first-year writing. She edits for Serpent Club Press, and is currently working on her first poetry chapbook, "From Bethlehem."

Nancy Cook grew up in Cleveland and now lives in St Paul. She has been engaged in community-based law practice for almost twenty years and is a clinical legal educator, mentoring students in public interest law practice. Her work has recently appeared or is forthcoming in *Adventum, Eleventh Muse, Stringybark*, and *The Poet's Quest for God Anthology*. As a recent recipient of an Artists Initiative grant from the Minnesota State Arts Board, she will be hosting "Justice Stories" community writing workshops in the coming year.

Sean Thomas Dougherty is the author or editor of thirteen books including the forthcoming "All I Ask for Is Longing: Poems 1994 - 2014" (2014 BOA Editions), "Scything Grace" (2013 Etruscan Press), and "Sasha Sings the Laundry on the Line" (2010 BOA Editions). He works at a pool hall in Erie, PA.

Kim Geralds is a freelance writer, lavender farm manager, and teacher who has lived in the Detroit area all her life. She writes short stories, poems, and children's literature, and has been published in a local parent's magazine. Kim is an "Emerging Writer Member'" of Detroit Working Writers and is currently working on an historical novel set during the Civil War's Battle of Perrysville.

Justin Glanville is a writer and urban planner based in Cleveland. He is the author of *New to Cleveland: A Guide to (Re)Discovering the City*, and has also worked a city reporter for The Associated Press. His writing has also appeared in *Planning* magazine and the *Cleveland Plain Dealer*. For his fiction, he was the recipient of a 2012 Creative Workforce Fellowship from the Community Partnership for Arts and Culture.

Sarah Grey is a freelance writer and editor at Grey Editing LLC (www.greyediting.com; @greyediting) in the Fishtown section of Philadelphia. Her editing practice specializes in history, sociology, media studies, and fiction, as well as translated work; her writing has been published in *Grid, Motivos, Monthly Review*, and *International Socialist Review*, among others. On the rare occasions when she doesn't have her head buried in a manuscript, she spends time with her husband and daughter, knits, and fights the power. Sarah is originally from Cheswick, Pennsylvania, and is still a proud member of the Steeler Nation.

Wint Huskey lives in Philadelphia.

Marissa Johnson-Valenzuela is a writer, teacher, and sometimes DJ in Philadelphia. Her writing has received recognition from The Leeway Foundation and Hedgebrook, among others. She is currently working on an untitled novel, a short story collection, and editing *Dismantle: An Anthology of Writing from the VONA/Voices Writing Workshop* for the small press she co-founded, Thread Makes Blanket. Marissa teaches full-time at the Community College of Philadelphia, tutors for its REACH prisoner re-entry program, instructs Chicano Studies courses online for The University of Wyoming, and facilitates a Latino Studies correspondence course for inmates in PA through Address This!, a project of Books Through Bars Philadelphia.

Liz Kerr is a recent M.F.A. graduate from Arcadia University. Her story was inspired by her grandmother, Betty, who was a seamstress in Kensington's Quaker Lace factory. She is a co-founder of Franklin's Paine Skatepark Fund, a non-profit dedicated to building public skateboard parks in Philadelphia. She is a Democratic Committeewoman, an officer in the Ancient Order of Hibernians, and a Registered Nurse on the Heart Transplant team at Temple University Hospital. She and her husband, Pearse, have two children, Dana and Brendan, and one dog, Shane MacGowan.

David Lewitzky is a 72-year-old retired social worker and family therapist living out his sedentary life in the sad and funky Rust Belt city of Buffalo, NY. He has recent work in *Nimrod*, *Passages North*, *Tidal Basin Review*, and *Roanoke Review*, among others. He has work forthcoming in *Ardent*, *Future Cycle*, and *Clarion*, as well as other publications.

M. Angelo Mena is a writer born and raised in Lancaster County, Pennsylvania. He's released a volume of short stories entitled *Strangers: a Study* and wrote the screenplay for the feature film *Mount Joy* (www.mountjoymovie.com). He currently lives in Philadelphia where he is trying to finish his first novel, which he sometimes describes as incidental slapstick sci-fi. It should also be known that he is always on the hunt for an illustrator willing to collaborate on a children's book that is written and waiting. He can be found online at www.mangelomena.com.

Karla Linn Merrifield recently received the Dr. Sherwin Howard Award for the best poetry published in Weber—The Contemporary West in 2012. A seven-time Pushcart-Prize nominee and National Park Artist-in-Residence, she has had 300+ poems appear in dozens of journals and anthologies. She has nine books to her credit, the newest of which chronicles the American West: "Lithic Scatter and Other Poems" (Mercury Heartlink). She is assistant editor and poetry book reviewer for *The Centrifugal Eye* (www.centrifugaleye.com). Visit her blog, Vagabond Poet, at www.karlalinn.blogspot.com.

Liz Moore is the author of the novels *The Words of Every Song* (Random House/Broadway Books, 2007) and *Heft* (W.W. Norton, 2012), along with works of short fiction and creative nonfiction that have been published in print and online in venues such as *The New York Times*, *Tin House*, *Narrative Magazine*, *The Tottenville Review*, and *The Drum*. She is also a professor of writing at Holy Family University in Philadelphia, where she lives. Her third novel is forthcoming from W.W. Norton.

Robert Tell's poetry and other work have appeared in many periodicals. A full length poetry book, "Bard Memorial Hospital," as well as Tell's novels, memoir, stories and poetry are widely available in both print and e-book editions. Originally from Brooklyn, and educated at Columbia University, Tell now lives and writes in Michigan and Florida. He nurtured his creative writing habit while working as a health care executive and professor. More information about Tell and his work can be found on his website: www.bobtell.com.

Christopher Wink is a journalist who enjoys exploring the fiction of stories he cannot know. By day, he is the editor of Technical.ly, a network of local technology news sites and events, including April's Philly Tech Week. The Temple University graduate lives in the Fishtown neighborhood of Philadelphia's Riverwards. He writes frequently on his personal blog, www.christopherwink.com, and tweets a lot @christopherwink.

Jeffrey Joseph Ziga is an Adult Video News (AVN) Award-Nominated Musician; Ice Cream Entrepreneur & Salesman; Writer; Comedy Enthusiast; Amateur Roastmaster; Business and Prank Artist; Vinyl Record & Cassette Tape Collector; Pantera T-Shirt Collector & Fan; Beavis & Butt-Head Archivist & Spokesperson; and whatever else. He has a sandwich named after him at a downtown establishment and once survived rolling sideways down a hill in van accident while in the Czech Republic. When he grows up, he wants to marry Daria.

Artists

Cindy La Ferle's mixed-media pieces have been exhibited in juried competitions throughout southeast Michigan. A graduate of Michigan State University, she's also a nationally published journalist. Her essay collection, Writing Home, won four awards for creative nonfiction. Her background in literature informs her artwork, whether she's altering a field guide to honor Thoreau or creating a mixed-media assemblage that evokes a carnival from a Ray Bradbury novel. La Ferle recycles old books, costume jewelry, rusted hardware, and fabric remnants. She believes that broken or damaged things have an irresistible patina and mystique -- and honors the back stories they bring to her artwork.

Amanda Gallant is a soft sculpture and illustration artist who hails from Ben Franklin's neck of the woods in Philadelphia. She lives in a very small house with a very large dog and creates most of her work on a very old barn table in her kitchen while drinking copious amounts of coffee.

Eyes Habit is a Philadelphia creative collective bent on crafting visual solutions that clarify important messages, generate awareness, and drive humans to make positive change. Over the past two years, Eyes Habit founders Mark Adams and Jason Killinger have helped create campaigns for various cultural and environmental organizations. Their uniquely personal screen printed maps of Philly neighborhoods can be found online and in various shops around town.

Julia Kuo is a Taiwanese-American freelance illustrator currently living in Chicago, IL. Her clients include the *New York Times*, Simon & Schuster, Capitol Records, Universal Music Group, and American Greetings. In addition to freelancing, Julia also teaches at Columbia College. She is part of The Nimbus Factory, a design boutique, and New to Cleveland, a partnership dedicated to creativity in the Rust Belt.

Danette Pascarella is a freelance photographer who has been living in Philadelphia for the past thirteen years. A former scientist, she turned to photography to indulge the artistic side of her brain to create images of everything from blushing brides to bashful babies to anything else that makes her happy. When she is not shooting, Danette likes to spend her time around the city drinking local hoppy beers, playing bocce, and going to Phillies games with friends.

K-Fai Steele is a Philadelphia-based illustrator and writer. Her book, *An Avian Allegory, the story of The Village of Arts and Humanities*, is due to be released in Fall 2013.

Jeffrey Stockbridge is a photographer based in Philadelphia, Pennsylvania. After graduating from Drexel University in 2005, Stockbridge has pursued many multi-year projects documenting the underbelly of inner-city life in Philadelphia. Concerned with the individuals quest to survive a harsh urban landscape, Stockbridge's photographs tell the stories of those affected by drug addiction, prostitution and abandonment. In 2010, Stockbridge was nominated for the Taylor-Wessing Photographic Portrait Prize at The National Portrait Gallery in London. He is a recipient of a Pennsylvania Council on the Arts Grant, an Independence Foundation Fellowship and a Center For Emerging Visual Artists Fellowship. His work has been featured in *The New York Times Magazine, Time* magazine and *The Sunday Telegraph*. He has exhibited nationally and internationally at The Wapping Project Bankside, The National Portrait Gallery London, The Philadelphia Museum of Art, The Institute of Contemporary Art at the University of Pennsylvania, The Fleisher Art Memorial, The Delaware Art Museum, and Galerie Huit in Arles, France.

Acknowledgments

Elizabeth Fuller, Librarian at the Rosenbach Library & guide to the almanacs of yore

Jason Killinger, in-house infographic artist & aesthetic soulmate

Angela Miles, Carpe Diem Construction Co., Art Director/layout scout

The artisans & merchants from Frankford Avenue and beyond who inspired us to make this almanac

The workers at Thomson Shore who continue their mission to rid the world of poorly made books

Our friends in the Philadelphia literary scene: *Apiary Magazine, Hidden City Magazine, Gigantic Sequins* & our *Workshop Crew* who provided endless feedback and criticism to help guide us

Samantha Slade, website development

Our wonderful writers & artists whose work fills these pages

Our illustrious staff: *Linda Gallant, Kerry Boland, Jeannette Bordeau, Chloe Westman, Claire Margheim* & *Nic Esposito*

Carl Cheeseman, sonic translation of "Ballad of August 27, 2012"

William Penn for the grand experiment of founding Philadelphia

Ben Franklin for giving us the model Almanac

Our friends and family who invested their time, love & money into this project

And finally, our deepest gratitude for the people who built these great cities, the people who are rebuilding the Rust Belt, and even the people who walked away from these cities. For without them, none of these stories would have been possible.